CORTÉS

and the Conquest of the Aztec Empire in World History

Titles *in World History*

**Cinqué of the *Amistad*
and the Slave Trade
in World History**
0-7660-1460-6

**Commodore Perry
Opens Japan to Trade
in World History**
0-7660-1462-2

**Cortés and the Conquest
of the Aztec Empire in
World History**
0-7660-1395-2

**Julius Caesar and
Ancient Rome
in World History**
0-7660-1461-4

**King Henry VIII
and the Reformation
in World History**
0-7660-1615-3

**Lenin and the
Russian Revolution
in World History**
0-7660-1464-9

**Leonardo da Vinci and
the Renaissance
in World History**
0-7660-1401-0

**Mahatma Gandhi and
India's Independence
in World History**
0-7660-1398-7

**Nelson Mandela and
Apartheid in World
History**
0-7660-1463-0

**Philip II and Alexander
the Great Unify Greece
in World History**
0-7660-1399-5

**Pizarro and the
Conquest of the Incan
Empire in World History**
0-7660-1396-0

**Robespierre and the
French Revolution
in World History**
0-7660-1397-9

**Stanley and Livingstone
and the Exploration of
Africa in World History**
0-7660-1400-2

CORTÉS
and the Conquest
of the Aztec Empire
in World History

Charles Flowers

Enslow Publishers, Inc.

40 Industrial Road	PO Box 38
Box 398	Aldershot
Berkeley Heights, NJ 07922	Hants GU12 6BP
USA	UK

http://www.enslow.com

*For Genaro Ahuatl, Roy Sanchez, and their families in
Puebla, worthy heirs today of Cuauhtémoc.*

Library of Congress Cataloging-in-Publication Data

Flowers, Charles.
    Cortes and the conquest of the Aztec Empire in world history / Charles
Flowers.
        p. cm. — (In world history)
    Includes bibliographical references and index.
    ISBN 0-7660-1395-2
    1. Cortes, Hernan, 1485–1547—Juvenile literature. 2. Mexico—
History—Conquest, 1519–1540—Juvenile literature. 3. Montezuma II,
Emperor of Mexico, ca. 1480–1520—Juvenile literature. 4. Aztecs—
History—Juvenile literature.   I. Title. II. Series.
    F1230.C835F56   2001
    972'.02'092--dc21
                                                                00-010309

Printed in the United States of America

10 9 8 7 6 5 4 3 2 1

To Our Readers: All Internet Addresses in this book were active and appropriate
at the time we went to press. Any comments or suggestions can be sent by e-mail
to Comments@enslow.com or to the address on the back cover.

Illustration Credits: © Corel Corporation, pp. 9, 15, 41, 44, 45, 52, 58,
66, 68, 75, 79, 110, 112, 117; Courtesy of the John Carter Brown Library
at Brown University, pp. 37, 48, 51; Cristoph Weiditz, *Das Tracthenbuch*,
1529, p. 26; Enslow Publishers, Inc., pp. 6, 23, 31, 99; Father Diego
Duran, *Historia de las Indias de Nueva Espana*, in the Biblioteca
National, Madrid, p. 21; Laurie Platt Winfrey, Inc., p. 90; Library of
Congress, p. 35; Reproduced from the *Dictionary of American Portraits*,
Published by Dover Publications, Inc., in 1967, p. 115; Zelia Nuttall, ed.,
The Codex Nuttall: A Picture Manuscript from Ancient Mexico (New York:
Dover Publications, Inc., 1975), p. 11.

Cover Illustration: Library of Congress (Hernán Cortés Portrait);
© Digital Vision Ltd. (Background).

Contents

Author's Note. 6

1 The Year of One Reed 7

2 The Great Speaker. 17

3 A Minor Noble 25

4 The City of Dreams 39

5 The Place of
White Herons 50

6 A Harsh Life. 60

7 The Fifth World Dies 73

8 The Gods Meet. 82

9 The Great Collapse. 97

10 Almost Forgotten. 109

Timeline 119

Chapter Notes 121

Further Reading 125

Internet Addresses. 126

Index . 7

Author's Note

The story of the Aztec Empire's defeat by Spanish soldiers is filled with excitement and mystery. But there are many gaps and contradictions in the historical record. Most of what is known was written by clergymen who traveled with the Spanish, or by the conquerors, who wanted to defend their actions. Many experts believe much of the history was written by the victors for their own purposes. Most of the Aztec's own picture-writing was destroyed.

Some Spanish clergymen did try to learn the story from the Aztec themselves. But did the Aztec reveal the truth to their conquerors? Did every writer carefully write the story? If some of the details may be incorrect or incomplete, the main story is perfectly clear: A small group of Spanish soldiers, quick to make allies with enemies of the Aztec, somehow defeated and destroyed one of the greatest empires in all of human history.

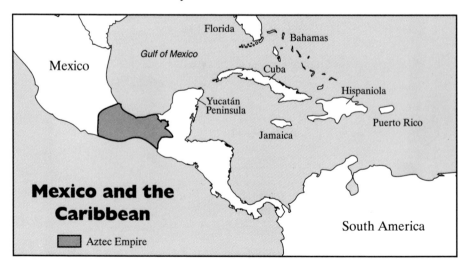

Mexico and the Caribbean

Chapter 1

The Year of One Reed

The earth has only been lent to us.
Tomorrow, or the day after,
The giver of life will beckon us to his home.

—From an Aztec poem[1]

Tenochtitlán was the glittering, thriving capital of a great empire in the year 1518. But its ruler, Montezuma II, the wise and powerful fifty-year-old emperor of the Aztec, kept hearing strange and frightening reports. Men with skin of stone and white faces had appeared in villages north of the mountains that protected the Valley of Mexico. They sat upon tame beasts and could kill a human instantly by pointing with a stick. Their large savage dogs were known to follow orders to tear into a human enemy's throat.

These strangers, a band of Spaniards under the leadership of Hernán Cortés, a minor noble, had the advantage of European technology. The Aztec had never seen steel armor or guns that fired death-dealing bullets. The horse had been extinct in America for thousands of years. These military advantages, it later turned out, were only effective on an open battlefield. They would not be so important when the Spanish invaders were outnumbered within city walls.

But in the terrible disaster to follow, the Spaniards, known as conquistadors, enjoyed another advantage: Montezuma, his priests, and his people had been terrified by ancient prophecies and eerie events. In the following year—1519, or the Year of One Reed—the god of the Morning Star—Quetzalcoatl—was predicted to appear in Mexico. The Aztec wondered if the strange beings were sent by him. They even wondered whether Cortés might be the god himself.

The Destiny of an Empire

The Aztec believed that their fate could always be read in the heavens, and they anxiously scanned the skies for clues. Suddenly, according to accounts written long afterward, there was an unusual number of eclipses. For more than a year, a comet bright enough to be seen in daylight blazed above Tenochtitlán. The planet Venus, sacred to Quetzalcoatl, cast a shadow on the sun, as it does only once every three hundred years.

It was said that two-headed men appeared in the capital, then mysteriously disappeared. The waters of Lake Texcoco, which surrounded the island capital,

Quetzalcoatl, often depicted as a plumed serpent, was one of the most important Aztec gods.

boiled furiously with unexplained waves. And Princess Butterfly, Montezuma's beloved aunt, fell into a trance and had a bloody vision: She saw the men with skins of stone killing thousands, including her nephew, before burning the city of Tenochtitlán to the ground. Because these stories were not recorded until years later, some might have been created by the defeated Aztec to explain how so few Spaniards could have conquered them. Still, they show the sense of fear that fell over the empire with the arrival of the Spaniards.

The Aztec religion did not offer much hope to fight their fears. According to ancient legend, four suns had been created and destroyed before the Aztec people appeared in the Valley of Mexico. They were now living beneath the Fifth Sun, which would someday burn out like the others.

The Aztec believed that no human could prevent this destiny. It was part of the natural cycle of life. Montezuma—whose name meant "he who rules by his great seriousness" in the Aztec language, Nahuatl— became deeply depressed.[2] "I shall be the last ruler of this land," he predicted.[3]

Still, some thought that the sun could be kept alive and the gods satisfied by offering more human sacrifices to the gods. A greater number of enemy captives, slaves, and other helpless people would be sacrificed in religious rituals. The Aztec believed that the blood streaming from their bodies would feed the sun.

Companions of the Sun

According to the Spanish observers, most sacrificial victims willingly climbed the steep steps of the great pyramid temples to the high altars where priests waited to kill them. Often, they were given a special potion with many ingredients blended with pulque, an alcoholic drink, to numb their fears. Or they ate dried peyote, a kind of mind-altering cactus that produced fantastic, brightly colored visions.

Yet many Aztec climbed bravely and even eagerly to their deaths.[4] They expected to be rewarded in the afterlife for feeding the gods with their blood.

The Aztec believed human sacrifice was essential to their survival. Sometimes the Aztec priests gave the intended victims drugs or drinks to conquer their fear before they were led to the altar.

The Spaniards saw for themselves how deeply the Aztec held this faith. After conquering the capital, they freed a young man who had promised to give his life on the altar. Far from being grateful, he secretly gathered his close friends together and begged them to sacrifice him in a religious ritual at a small temple outside town. His friends agreed. The Spanish conquerors were amazed.

No one knows when human sacrifice began in Mexico, but the Aztec copied the ritual from other

Source Document

The ordinary manner of sacrificing was, to open the stomake of him that was sacrificed, and having pulled out his heart halfe alive, they tumbled the man down the stairs of the Temple, which were all imbrewed and defiled with bloud: And to make it more plain, sixe Sacrificers being appointed to this dignitie, came into the place of Sacrifice, foure to hold the hands and feet of him that should be sacrificed, the fift to hold his head, and the sixt to open his stomake, and to pull out the heart of the sacrificed.[5]

A missionary named José de Acosta described the ritual of Aztec human sacrifice.

groups native to the area. By the time of Montezuma, there were many types of special sacrifice. To bring rain to grow corn, or maize, an essential food in the ancient Americas, a young child was beaten until it wept and was then drowned in a river. The child's tears were supposed to produce the February rains that began the growing season. When the first maize shoots broke through the ground in June, a young woman was beheaded so that her blood could fertilize the life-giving plants.

One very elaborate ritual shows how carefully each part of a sacrifice was planned in order to please the gods. Each year, a handsome young man—an Aztec or an enemy warrior captured on the battlefield—was chosen to play the role of the powerful war god Tezcatlipoca. He was served by eight priests, who treated him like a living deity, and was given every luxury. Four beautiful young Aztec girls became his wives. At the end of the year, the priests killed him on an altar. Then another good-looking captive took his place.

Lord of the Smoking Mirror

In addition to other fears, the story of the god Tezcatlipoca, also known as the Lord of the Smoking Mirror, may have weighed heavily upon Montezuma's heart as Cortés and his Spanish conquistadors approached. The problem was both religious and political.

According to legend, when the Aztec came to power in the Valley of Mexico, they probably destroyed an older people known as the Toltec, who worshipped Quetzalcoatl. The Toltec believed that this god came down from the sky to rule them and act as the priest of their religion. During a ritual feast, a sly goddess tricked him into eating too much of her "food of the gods," a sacred hallucinogenic mushroom. While he was in a drugged stupor, he committed a sin.

Horrified that he had betrayed his mission, Quetzalcoatl left all his rich possessions behind and traveled east to the Caribbean Sea. He made a raft from snakeskins and sailed toward the rising sun. Suddenly, his small craft burst into flames and his heart magically rose into the sky, becoming the bright star we know as the planet Venus. He also became known as the Feathered Serpent. He was especially associated with the bright green feathers of the high-flying quetzal, a bird found in rain forests to the southeast of Mexico. The other part of his name, *coatl*, means snake.

The Aztec honored this Toltec god, who was the patron of poetry and medical knowledge. They believed he was also responsible for causing the sun to rise each day.

But the most important of the Aztec gods was Tezcatlipoca, the warrior god known as the eagle. It was Tezcatlipoca who kept their empire powerful. In Toltec times, he was less important than Quetzalcoatl, but the Aztec considered him their high god and

A wall of a temple to Quetzalcoatl is seen here in ruins.

patron. The ruler's political authority was affirmed solely by Tezcatlipoca. Thrones were covered with jaguar skin because the god was associated with the predator. Tezcatlipoca was a fierce, often violent deity, not at all a loving father. Even so, most Aztec hymns were sung to him, calling him the "Giver of Life."[6] His footprint could be seen in the night sky as the constellation now called Ursa Major, or the Great Bear. The combative Tezcatlipoca and the kindly Quetzalcoatl could be considered rivals for the soul of the Aztec people.

Montezuma and his priests might have worried that Quetzalcoatl was returning, as some prophets supposedly predicted, to defeat Tezcatlipoca and punish the Aztec for destroying the Toltec. Quetzalcoatl had gone into exile in the east; the Spaniards had sailed from the east to reach the Caribbean coast of Mexico. The Aztec had come out of unknown lands to defeat the Toltec. It looked as if the Spaniards were also coming from mysterious lands to challenge the Aztec.

Chapter 2

The Great Speaker

As many Spaniards would later admit, Montezuma was an intelligent, hardworking, and courageous leader. He had won many battles against other native groups, but he was an even more outstanding ruler in peacetime. He made certain that everyone obeyed the law. In fact, the nobility was punished more severely for some crimes because the nobles were supposed to set an example for the common people. Montezuma was known to confine crooked judges in animal cages before having them executed. He tried to fulfill the royal and godlike image described by the elders at the crowning of any new ruler: "Now thou art deified. Although thou art human, as are we, although thou art our son, our younger brother, no more art thou human, as are we. . . . [T]hou speakest in a strange tongue to the god, the lord of the near, of the high."[1]

A Wise Leader

But despite his wisdom, honesty, and sincere concern for his people, Montezuma was true to his proud heritage as the eighth all-powerful emperor to rule the Aztec. He was famous for ruling "with fear, not affection."[2] As both a former general and high priest, he knew the history and religion of the nation well. He made certain that all sacrifices and other religious rites strictly followed the ancient codes. Once, after mercilessly putting down a revolt in the province of Oaxaca, he had twelve thousand rebels sacrificed in thanks to Tezcatlipoca. He was simply honoring tradition. The previous emperor, Montezuma's uncle Ahuítzotl, once sacrificed twenty thousand captives, an exhausting ritual that took four days and fourteen pyramid altars to complete.

Still, a Spanish priest would describe Montezuma as "modest, virtuous and generous, and with all the virtues which one could look for in a good prince."[3] His wavy black hair, light brown skin, and slender limbs were typical of his people, but his head was unusually large and his nostrils rather flat.

Above all, he was extremely polite, speaking softly and carefully to even the least important of his subjects. Imitating him, the Aztec and their neighbors valued courtesy, especially to strangers. Even their table manners were strict. For example, women were not allowed to speak during meals, even as they served food in their own homes. Other rules make sense even today. Fathers told their sons, "Do not gossip . . . if you be rude, you will get along with none."[4]

The Spaniards Arrive

The loud, rude Spanish shocked and puzzled the Aztec. At the same time, the behavior of the Aztec often gave the invaders the wrong impression: Gentle speech and good manners did not mean that Montezuma's people would be afraid to fight to the death if the need arose.

The first meeting between Spaniards and the Aztec in 1518 seemed to go well. Spanish explorers under Juan de Grijalva had come to Mesoamerica from Cuba, looking for gold and places to settle and making contact with the natives of the region. The Spaniards had not traveled as far as the lands of the Aztec, but when they heard of the explorers' arrival, the Aztec sent messengers to see the Spaniards. Acting like a host welcoming an invited guest, Montezuma sent nobles with gifts to greet the strangers, whose ships lay at anchor on the coast near today's Mexican city of Veracruz. Objects made of fine gold and rare feathers were sent to prove Montezuma's grandeur. Beautiful costumes for priests to wear at services honoring the gods were included among the presents. These holy objects suggested that the gods of the Aztec would protect them from enemies. A wide variety of foods, from turkey to maize to chocolate, many of which the Spaniards had not tried before, showed that Montezuma had an empire that covered many different lands.

In return, the Spaniards gave the Aztec gifts of bread, biscuits, and cheap bead necklaces. They also introduced the Aztec to wine. One of the Spaniards said, "Go in peace. We go first to Castile [Spain], but we shall not delay in returning to Mexico."[5]

Back in Tenochtitlán, the emperor could only guess at the future. He did not yet know that his rich gifts, far from frightening the Spaniards with his great power, would tempt them to return and seize his wealth.

Meanwhile, the king of a neighboring land bet Montezuma that the Aztec Empire would soon fall. To settle the wager, the kings played an ancient ball game. Montezuma won two rounds but lost the last three. Later, he looked into a mirror made of obsidian, a dark black stone, for a vision. This was the type of magic mirror referred to in the god Tezcatlipoca's name, Lord of the Smoking Mirror. In its dim reflections, according to a later report, Montezuma may have seen the same shocking scenes that his aunt had described.

Soon Montezuma became dangerous to those around him. He killed the families of fortune-tellers who refused to explain what the future held for Tenochtitlán. Those who bravely predicted the worst were sometimes never seen again.

Montezuma, as the religious leader of his people, was supposed to be most adept at reading the meaning of such signs as comets in the sky.

The Spaniards had promised to return soon. As Montezuma knew, they would probably come back in the fateful Year of One Reed—1519.

Smoking Mountain

In November 1519, the Spaniards under Hernán Cortés climbed through a fragrant pine forest to a chilly mountain pass, some thirteen thousand feet high, between two sleeping volcanoes southeast of Tenochtitlán. As they shivered beneath the snow-covered peaks, which rose another mile above and were known in Nahuatl as Popocatepetl and Ixtaccihuatl, they saw a vast valley surrounded by rocky mountains and warmed by the sun. Maguey cactus plants, which were used to make pulque, covered the ground in all directions.[6]

Tenochtitlán, with its two hundred fifty thousand inhabitants, gleamed about five miles in the distance, an island city in beautiful Lake Texcoco, about seventy-four hundred feet above sea level. The lake waters, which were actually five lakes linked together, reflected the colorful name of their divine caretaker, the lady of the "jade skirt."

Connecting lakes and neighboring towns were framed by fertile farmlands outlined by rows of willow trees. Every available acre was in use, because in Montezuma's day the area was so highly populated that no land could be left unfarmed. He wanted the national storehouses fully stocked in preparation for the droughts that often struck the Valley of Mexico. Known as he who commands, Montezuma was the national father. Like all Aztec fathers, "he regulates, distributes with care, establishes order."[7] The well-tended farms were important to the nation. Except for small private gardens in Tenochtitlán, food had to be transported from the valley to feed the island capital. Montezuma's official inspectors probably told farmers which crops would be most useful.

To the perhaps four hundred Spanish warriors, the dramatic scenery was unfamiliar. Perhaps none of them had ever seen a volcano, and Popocatepetl was

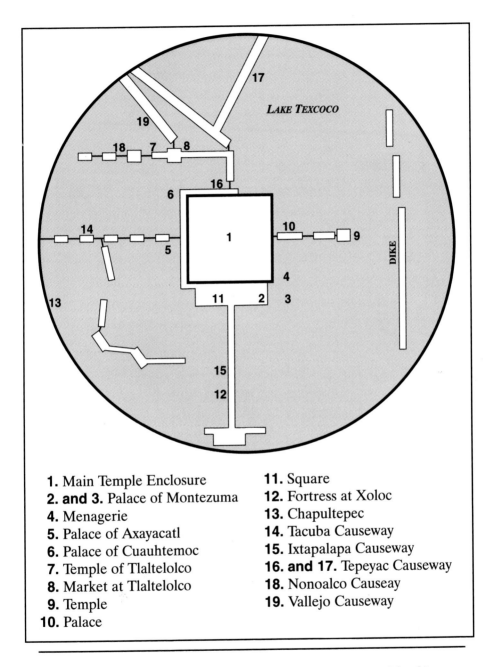

1. Main Temple Enclosure
2. and 3. Palace of Montezuma
4. Menagerie
5. Palace of Axayacatl
6. Palace of Cuauhtemoc
7. Temple of Tlaltelolco
8. Market at Tlaltelolco
9. Temple
10. Palace
11. Square
12. Fortress at Xoloc
13. Chapultepec
14. Tacuba Causeway
15. Ixtapalapa Causeway
16. and 17. Tepeyac Causeway
18. Nonoalco Causeay
19. Vallejo Causeway

The Aztec had built their capital city, Tenochtitlán, on an island in the center of Lake Texcoco.

smoking and throwing up hot rock. They had heard that they were greatly outnumbered by the armies in the distance, even though they had about one hundred fifty Indian porters from Cuba and had picked up several hundred to several thousand Indian allies who hated Aztec rule. In all the world, perhaps only Naples, the great seaport in Italy, and Constantinople, the capital of the Ottoman Empire in Turkey, were as large as the busy capital city of Tenochtitlán. The Spaniards had found out that Aztec power extended from the Atlantic to the Pacific, from the deserts of the north to the jungles of the south.

But if his men were fearful or awed, Cortés was excited. He may even have recalled to himself one of his favorite Latin mottoes, *"Fortes Fortuna adiuvat"* (Fortune favors the brave).[8] The magnificent sight on the plains below was just what he hoped to find after hearing about Montezuma's gifts to the Spaniards at Veracruz in 1518. This was his chance to become one of the richest and most famous men in Europe.

Chapter 3

A Minor Noble

To his own countrymen back in Spain, Hernán Cortés was not very impressive. Only five feet four inches tall, he was thin and bowlegged. His smallish head seemed even smaller atop a barrel-thick chest. His skin was unusually pale, set off by reddish-brown long hair and a scraggly beard. His eyes were notably "mild and grave."[1] But this average-looking man, like other conquerors in the New World, had boldly bet his life and the lives of his men on this risky adventure.

Cortés ignored the clear orders of his superior, the governor of Cuba. (Cuba was the headquarters of the new, expanding Spanish Empire in the Americas.) The governor told Cortés to return and make a report rather than mount an invasion in Mexico. Brashly, Cortés instead had nine of his twelve Spanish ships beached on the Caribbean sands and stripped of their

Hernán Cortés hoped to win fame and wealth through his brave expeditions in America.

equipment, to make certain his men could not turn back and sail for home. He later wrote about their reaction: "on this [they] abandoned any hope of leaving the land."[2]

Background of a Conquistador

Younger than Montezuma, Cortés was probably between thirty-four and thirty-six years old. The Spaniard had been working hard to make a fortune since his teens. He had grown up in Spain in the town of Medellín, the son of a minor noble, or *hidalgo*, described at the time as "rather poor."[3]

The Cortés family owned small wheatfields, a vineyard, beehives, a mill, and rental properties. But as aristocrats they felt they deserved better. Their son wanted wealth—and much more—from the world. He once wrote his father, "I look on it as better to be rich in fame than in goods."[4] Only about eight years old when Christopher Columbus made his first trip to America, Cortés may have heard fantastic stories soon afterward about the strange new lands across the Atlantic Ocean.

When he was about twelve, Cortés was sent to live with relatives in Salamanca, where he probably prepared to become a lawyer by taking classes in grammar and ancient Latin. According to friends, he was a fair student but a much better swordsman and gambler. His father had fought in many battles, and Hernán must have heard stories at home about the true nature of combat in the field.[5]

Source Document

Christopher Columbus, after discovering and conquering the said Islands and Continent in the said ocean, or any of them, shall be our Admiral of the said Islands and Continent you shall discover and conquer; and that you shall be our Admiral, Vice-Roy, and Governour in them. . . .[6]

Christopher Columbus was granted enormous privileges by the Spanish king and queen for his achievements in America. Cortés hoped to receive similar acclaim.

By about age seventeen, Cortés had made up his mind: He would seize his fortune on the battlefield. For a while, he thought of joining the Spanish armies fighting in Italy, but he finally decided that his best chances lay in America, then known to Europeans as the West Indies. Several opportunities to cross the Atlantic fell through. At last, when he was about twenty-two years old, he paid to sail to the island of Hispaniola, which had come under the control of Spain after many bloody battles with the local Indians.

Experiences in a New World

Hernán Cortés's first years in the New World, despite the help of family friends in high places, were not especially profitable. He may have been given a farm with American Indians to work it. He used his Latin skills to do paperwork as a secretary, or *escribano*, for the Spanish government that ran the island. He used his talent for soldiering in his country's conquest of Cuba, the largest island in the West Indies, and began to prosper there, raising cattle and searching for gold in riverbeds.

But he was far from satisfied. Like other ambitious Spaniards in the Americas, he leapt at every opportunity to improve his fortunes. Fortunately, he had served with distinction under Diego Velázquez in the conquest of Cuba. When Velázquez was appointed governor of the island, he chose Cortés to lead an expedition to the Yucatán, a peninsula in southeast Mexico.

Officially, Cortés's mission was to tell the Indian inhabitants of the region that Charles V, the emperor of Spain, was now their ruler and that they were expected to convert from their own religion to the Roman Catholic Church. Cortés was also to report on the foods grown by the natives, bring back gold, and look for the Spaniards of the 1518 Grijalva expedition, who had not been heard from.

Cortés rounded up six ships for his expedition, paying a third to half the costs out of his own pocket. He left Cuba for the Mexican mainland on November 18, 1518. Eventually, he would have a total of twelve ships and some five hundred thirty Spanish soldiers under his command.

Piracy to Conquest

Unofficially, this expedition was little more than a money-making venture, or even piracy. Cortés was careful to treat the Mayan Indians of the Yucatán with courtesy. Once a mighty empire, the Maya had suffered civil wars and other disasters in the century before the Spanish arrived. Their art, religion, calendar, and other great achievements influenced other groups in Mesoamerica. But Cortés was more interested in present opportunities. He was constantly on the lookout for products to exploit, especially precious metals. Whenever he was given small presents of local gold, he promptly asked for more.

Soon, the Maya attacked the Spaniards, but the guns of the Europeans drove the natives back. Cortés began conquering villages and demanding information about the gold and silver that meant so much to all European invaders. These metals did not interest the Maya. They said, however, that other Indians who lived to the west did collect them. They might have meant the Aztec. Or they might simply have been trying to get Cortés to leave them alone.

But more important to Cortés's success than gold was the appearance of a young Mayan woman who would become famous as "Marina." The daughter of a Mayan noble, she was born as Malintzin. She was sold into slavery when her father died and was given to the Spaniards as a gift. Often described as "beautiful as a goddess," Marina became invaluable to Cortés.[7] In childhood, she had learned Nahuatl, the language of the Aztec. In this language, there is no *r* sound, so she became known to Montezuma's spies and messengers as Malina. She was gifted as a translator. She also knew how to shape Cortés's words to make him seem even more determined and fearsome than he was. In the centuries after her death, she became known as *La Llorona*, the "official ghost" of Mexico.[8] For helping the Spaniards against her own people, she was doomed to wander through the night, weeping for the Indians killed by the Spaniards.

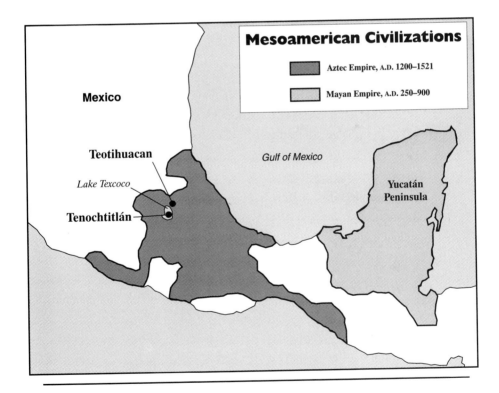

Mesoamerican Civilizations

Aztec Empire, A.D. 1200–1521

Mayan Empire, A.D. 250–900

Mexico

Teotihuacan

Lake Texcoco

Tenochtitlán

Gulf of Mexico

Yucatán Peninsula

Ancient Mesoamerica was home to many groups of American Indians, but the Maya and the Aztec were the dominant powers.

On Good Friday, 1519, Cortés landed near what is now Veracruz. As had happened with Grijalva the year before, a messenger from Montezuma appeared and gave the Spaniards gifts. Describing himself as an ambassador from the king of Spain, Cortés asked whether the Aztec emperor had any gold. Not understanding that telling the truth could be dangerous, the Aztec messenger admitted that his ruler had much of the yellow metal.

Worse, Montezuma soon sent Cortés amazing treasures, including jungle animals carved from gold and precious jewels. The most famous gifts were two wooden disks—one covered with gold and carved with symbols of the sun, the other covered with silver to represent the moon. The thirty-five-pound sun disk was about six and a half feet in diameter. These gifts sealed the doom of the Aztec Empire. They proved to Cortés that the Aztec had a wide range of resources and treasure.

After receiving this information about the native people and their resources, Cortés's fellow Spaniards wanted to return to Cuba, as their government had ordered. Cortés, however, cleverly argued that their king would want them to seize the opportunity to start a colony in this rich, exotic land. To those who thought he was only seeking treasure for himself, he promised to forget about gold and devote his attention to serving the king and God. The friars (clergymen) on the mission, and possibly some of the military officers, truly believed that God wanted them to save the Aztec

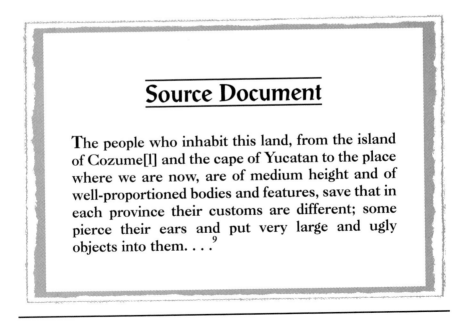

from eternal damnation by converting them to Christianity. They also believed that they were serving Emperor Charles V by bringing a new land under Spanish control.

They established the city of Villa Rica de la Vera Cruz (*Vera Cruz* means True Cross). Cortés persuaded his men to elect him mayor and captain general of the territories they intended to capture.

Thus, without the approval of any Spanish official in the colonies or in Spain, Cortés began the road to conquest. He showed that he was as daring as other conquerors who would succeed in the New World. Some outraged Spaniards, especially the governor of

Source Document

The people who inhabit this land, from the island of Cozume[l] and the cape of Yucatan to the place where we are now, are of medium height and of well-proportioned bodies and features, save that in each province their customs are different; some pierce their ears and put very large and ugly objects into them. . . .[9]

In his first letter to the Spanish Crown, Cortés described the people he was encountering on his arrival in Mexico.

Cuba and some fellow officers who felt Cortés lacked the proper social background, believed he had actually stolen his power. But he answered that he needed complete control in order to conquer the Aztec Empire for the glory of the Spanish nation and the Christian religion.

The Road of Fate

The dangers of the march toward Tenochtitlán allowed the Spaniards to sharpen their military skills. East of the Aztec capital lay Tlaxcala, or "the place of maize cakes" (tortillas), a city that Montezuma's forces had never been able to subdue. These Indians greatly outnumbered the Spanish soldiers but were soundly defeated twice. Recognizing that the tide of power was about to turn in Mexico, the Tlaxcalans joined with Cortés to fight against their Aztec enemies. With their great numbers and their knowledge of the land, these allies would become invaluable to Cortés.

After two weeks in this friendly city, the mixed band of Spaniards and Indian allies traveled next to Cholula, whose inhabitants supported Montezuma. These Indians tried to trap and kill the Spaniards but Cortés discovered their plan and slaughtered many of their leaders and warriors in a single bloody afternoon. Some six thousand Indians were butchered in about five hours, thanks to the effectiveness of the Spaniards' steel swords. Now only the rumbling

A twentieth-century Mexican artist depicted the violence and chaos of the Spanish conquest of the Aztec Empire.

volcanoes lay between the conquistadors and the Aztec capital.

But the Spaniards had learned important lessons. Because it was the end of summer, the Indian men were working hard to harvest crops. They could not focus on repelling the Spanish invaders and their allies. Nor had the natives ever approached warfare with the same aims, battlefield methods, and weapons as these strangers from across the sea.

The Spaniards quickly saw that the Indian armies did not use teamwork on the battlefield. Instead, each warrior tried on his own to capture an enemy to be sacrificed later on the high altars of the war god. The warriors would be rewarded for each man they captured. But the Europeans used techniques first developed in ancient Greece and refined in ancient

Rome. They lined up in tight, armored rows and mowed down their disorganized Indian opponents.

Conquistadors on horseback, protected by steel or padded cotton armor from Indian arrows and sling-stones, could fight with lances or swords as their horses plunged into the thick of the enemy. The Indians had no shield against the light cannons and muskets of the invaders.

When soldiers met face to face, the Spaniards' swords and pikes—long metal staffs with sharp steel blades at the tip—were much deadlier than Indian clubs tipped with obsidian. Spanish soldiers killed so quickly and cruelly, not even sparing small children, that the Indians called them *popolucas*, or "barbarians."

Cortés did not mind this nickname. He hoped that the Aztec and other Indians would be too terrified to fight when they learned that his conquistadors cut off their victims' noses, ears, and other body parts. At the same time, he tried to hide the deaths of his horses on the battlefield. They were buried deep in the ground by night so that the Indians—who had never seen horses before—would not realize that they could be killed.

Meanwhile, just as rapidly as Cortés was learning firsthand about how the Indians fought, Montezuma's spies were racing back home to report on the overpowering Spanish warriors. Each leader was creating a plan to outwit the other, when the time came. Each

An artist's depiction of the extreme cruelty of the Spanish conquistadors toward the native population of Mexico.

tried to guess the weaknesses and strengths of the other side.

At the same time, the two men pretended that all would be peaceful. Cortés said he wanted to visit Tenochtitlán as a friend, and Montezuma promised to welcome Cortés into the capital as a guest. The Aztec began to prepare for the visit of guests who were already acting like conquerors.

Chapter 4

The City of Dreams

And some of our soldiers even asked whether the things that we saw were not a dream.

—Bernal Díaz del Castillo,
a conquistador under Cortés[1]

Fantastic and dreamlike to the Spanish invaders, Tenochtitlán was a very down-to-earth trading and political center to the Aztec. They called it the "place of the cactus fruit."[2] It was certainly beautiful, but it was most important as the heart of a huge, thriving kingdom. If Cortés could capture this capital, he would control the whole Aztec Empire.

Three causeways, or low roads with removable bridges, connected the twenty-five-hundred-acre island of Tenochtitlán to the mainland. A sturdy stone aqueduct brought fresh water from springs near the west bank of the lake. There were more canals than streets in the city, reminding the conquistadors and many later European visitors of the canals of Venice, Italy.

Scattered around the main island were smaller artificial islands, or *chinampas*, covered with maize and other crops. The bright green of these famous gardens—called "floating gardens," although they were actually attached to the muddy lake bottom— and the lush plants on the city's patios made a brilliant contrast with the white-painted, one-story adobe houses of the common people. Pinkish volcanic rock had been used to build some thirty or so large villas for noble families.

Pyramids with high altars rose throughout the city. Near the tallest and most monumental of these, the one-hundred-fifty-foot-high *Templo Mayor*, or Great Temple, many thousands of skulls from human sacrifices were displayed on seventy tall racks, or *tzompantli*. One European stopped counting the skulls at 136,000. Despite their own brutality in warfare, the Spaniards were horrified by the human sacrifices the Aztec practiced.

As Cortés gazed around the busy Aztec capital, he knew that he faced a huge challenge. No enemy had ever dared to attack Tenochtitlán, which could be cut off from the mainland by raising the movable bridges. For almost a century, the nearby lakeside kingdoms of Texcoco and Tlacopan had been united with the Aztec capital in the Triple Alliance. Each of the three city-states vowed to defend the others.

This wall of skulls at Templo Mayor showed the Spaniards just how important human sacrifice was to the Aztec people.

The Aztec people crowded close and smiled in welcome when the Spaniards entered the city, but Cortés knew that they would all die for their emperor if necessary. The able-bodied Aztec men outnumbered the conquistadors and their Tlaxcalan allies by perhaps a hundred to one.

Besides, Tenochtitlán could draw on forces from other parts of the empire, which stretched some three hundred fifty miles from the Pacific Ocean in the west to the Atlantic Ocean in the east. The total area under Aztec control, thanks to Montezuma's skill in battle and politics, was about one hundred twenty-five thousand square miles. It included more than sixty cities and their states or provinces.

By contrast, Cortés and his small band could not rely on reinforcements from Cuba. No one was on the way to help them. It would take months for any messenger to sail to Cuba to ask for help. Yet, as Cortés walked toward the emperor's grand palace in the center of the city, he began to see that Tenochtitlán might be conquered as easily as the much smaller, weaker town of Cholula he had recently taken over. Cortés would have to take a big risk, but it was the chance of a lifetime. Like other conquering Europeans, he knew that capturing the Aztec ruler would be the most efficient way to gain control of his people.

Lifeblood of the Nation

The Spaniards knew that gold and silver were not the only riches to tempt a conqueror. The many small canoes gliding toward town on the lake and through the canals were piled high with fresh foods. Farming was the lifeblood of the Aztec Empire.

The Aztec did not have money, but traders came from all over ancient Mesoamerica with the most desirable crafts, clothing, tools, weapons, and decorations. In the bustling markets of teeming Tenochtitlán, where an estimated fifty thousand sellers and buyers appeared on market day, a visitor might see macaw and quetzal feathers, imported obsidian and flint, painted pottery, baskets, copper knives, turquoise, bells, and precious jade, which was much more highly valued by the Aztec than gold.

These goods and others had been brought by foot from every corner of the empire. The Aztec used wheels in toys but did not have wheeled carts. Other ancient American peoples who did not have horses or donkeys used large dogs to pull loads. The Aztec did not. Instead, the merchant traders hired porters to trudge across the burning deserts and up the cold mountain passes with fifty-pound loads on their backs. They carried as much as possible in order to make the journey worthwhile, typically logging about fifteen miles in a five-hour workday.

Under the rule of the Aztec emperors, many towns had developed their own special products, perhaps because a source of ore for metalworking or clay for ceramics was nearby. Montezuma and his generals expected traders to act as spies on faraway cities.

Arranged in fifty different sections, the market stalls offered foodstuffs from the Valley of Mexico such as maize, peppers, a variety of beans, tomatoes, avocados, and many types of squash. The maguey cactus was sold for food as well as for brewing pulque. From the southern coast of the Caribbean came pineapples, vanilla, honey, and cacao beans. These beans were the source of an unsweetened chocolate liquid so prized that only the nobility was allowed to drink it.

Many of these foods were unknown in Europe at the time. Cacao would soon be sent across the Atlantic

On sale at the Tenochtitlán market were all sorts of plants and animals. This flowering cactus was one plant that was native to ancient Mesoamerica.

in large, and profitable, volumes. Other items on view in the market would also help make the Spaniards rich later, despite the high cost of ocean transportation: tobacco, rubber, and lacquer, a shellac used for decoration or to prevent brass from tarnishing.

Not every item of food appealed to European tastes or was profitable to ship across the Atlantic. Along with the fruits and vegetables there were turkeys, quail, ducks, rabbits, geese, and even parrots to cook. There was also meat from a hairless breed of dog raised especially for eating. The maguey slug, an insect found on the cactus, was on display because the Aztec considered it delicious.

Cortés's men must have been dazzled by the sheer variety of decorative objects and colorful clothing brought by craftsmen to market. Fine jewelry such as finger rings and plugs for pierced lips was molded and hammered from gold, silver, and copper. These luxury items might have tinkling bells or tiny pendants attached. Strings of pearls were used as collars or necklaces. Prized jade, turquoise, and obsidian were carved into ornaments, ceremonial knives, and small figurines of animals or gods. Brooches were designed with religious symbols.

Aztec artisans made finely carved figures, both for sale at market and for religious purposes.

The featherwork that Montezuma had sent as gifts to the Spaniards at least twice before their arrival in his city was echoed in the red, green, yellow, and blue designs of cloaks, tall headdresses, and banners. The feathers were sewn or glued to cloth backings to make designs. At the height of the empire, so many thousands of brightly colored birds were kept in the capital for their feathers that some three hundred keepers were necessary to feed and care for them.

Whatever the Spaniards thought of these exotic wares, they surely grasped one obvious fact: These were objects made by hardworking craftsmen for the rich and powerful. In Tenochtitlán, there was a class system, just as there was in Spain. Aztec society was organized with a few noble families at the top and hundreds of thousands of common people at the bottom to work in the fields, serve in the armies, and create beautiful decorations for others. The small middle class was mostly made up of successful traders known as *pochteca.* As far as historians know, this system was accepted at all levels as the best way to keep the whole country orderly and peaceful.

Rigid but Effective

Although Montezuma was emperor for life and was considered a kind of god, he was required to seek the advice of a supreme council of nobles. This system helped ensure that the emperor would hear all sides of an issue and act in the best interests of his people. Four generals, each responsible for defending a quarter of the capital city, discussed military matters with Montezuma.

But above all of these advisors was the *cihuacoatl*, or "Snake Woman," a man who, as deputy emperor, actually managed the practical affairs of the kingdom. It is not clear why he was called "Snake Woman," but his other title, "chief of men," helps explain his importance. He was the supreme judge in the legal system. Elected by the council, which could unseat him whenever it chose, Snake Woman often acted as the nation's representative to other groups in peace or war. The Spaniards would soon learn to bargain with this official.

As the Europeans would expect, most of the nobility inherited their titles and wealth, which were backed by gifts of land from the emperor. The Aztec believed that the nobility deserved lives of privilege. Sometimes, an especially brave warrior or clever hunter would be rewarded with a noble title and given farmland captured by the national armies.

The rulers of kingdoms, called *tlatoani*, or "speakers," were regarded as the wisest men in public life. They met together as the members of Montezuma's supreme council. They were responsible for governing the provinces of the empire outside Tenochtitlán. Below them were the *teuctli*, or "lords," a respected class that produced judges, generals, and elected officials throughout the land. Members of the nobility never had to pay taxes.

A ritual dance being performed by Aztec nobles and priests.

Most people observed by the Spaniards, of course, were commoners, or the *macehualtin*. Each *macehual* was assigned to a ward known as a *calpulli*. In Tenochtitlán there were twenty wards, five for each of the city's four districts. It was the ward that gave commoners the right to inherit and farm a specific plot of land. This property remained in the family unless a farmer let it go to seed or died without leaving an heir. A hardworking macehual could make a very good living and even buy slaves to work his fields.

At the lowest rank in Aztec society, slaves, or *tlatlacotin*, came from many different circumstances. Some were enemy captives whose skills made them too valuable to be sacrificed. Others were criminals. These people were typically given to the victims of their thefts or other offenses. The poor sometimes sold themselves or their children into slavery. The Aztec did not treat slaves harshly, unless they were warriors captured in battle. Slaves were allowed to own property, including other slaves, and their own children were always born free under the law.

The organization of the many ranks of Aztec society had taken centuries to develop, but it was firmly set and stable by Montezuma's day. The hundreds of thousands of citizens of Tenochtitlán went about their business efficiently and capably. For that reason, no European visitor could possibly guess that this vast, well-run empire was born in myth and mystery, or that the Aztec had once been one of the poorest of many groups in the Valley of Mexico.

Chapter 5

The Place of White Herons

We shall proceed to establish ourselves and settle down, and we shall conquer all peoples of the universe.

—Huitzilopochtli, mythical Aztec leader[1]

The proud Aztec descended from a small wandering tribe. They carefully preserved the story of their origins. This history was a blend of legends, folktales, and religious belief that bound them together as a nation. It made them feel superior to all other Indian nations.

Origins of the Aztec

But the history was incomplete. The Aztec believed that they originally came from an island called Aztlan, or "the place of white herons." In fact, it inspired the name *Aztec*. This humble homeland, surrounded by reedbeds, was set in a freshwater lagoon somewhere north of the Valley of Mexico. The exact location had been forgotten. Experts today point toward several islands centered in mountain lakes in the northern regions of Mexico and also toward sites in the American Southwest.

The Aztec left their island on the orders of their leader Huitzilopochtli, who had a grand vision of their future in a land to the south. After he died, he was regarded as a god. His priests led his people through the deserts and mountains of Mexico for many years, always carrying a sacred idol in his image. Sometimes they settled down to farm and hunt in one location for two or three years. Sometimes they stayed for up to

Huitzilopochtli, the hummingbird, was one of the principal gods of the Aztec religion.

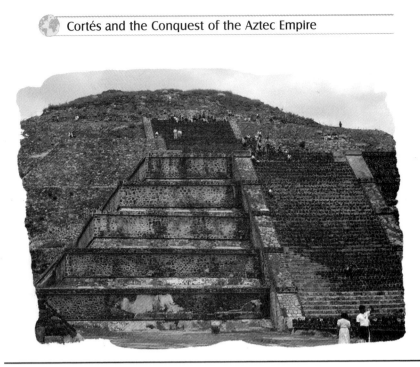

Many temples were built to honor Huitzilopochtli, the visionary Aztec leader worshipped as a god for inspiring his people to found a great empire.

two decades, building houses, ballcourts, and temples in honor of Huitzilopochtli.

But they could not settle permanently until they found a sacred place promised to them in a religious prophecy. As they searched over the years, they found "Curved Mountain," which was probably anywhere from sixty to one hundred eighty miles northeast of Tenochtitlán. Then they came to the ancient shrine known as Seven Caves and renewed their determination to discover the land of their prophecies.

At last, after about one hundred fifty years of travel, the original Aztec trudged to the rim of the fertile

Valley of Mexico in about A.D. 1250. Unfortunately, all the good land had already been seized by other groups. The Aztec were forced to try their luck on a bleak hillside next to a swamp in an area known as Chapultepec, or "place of the grasshopper."

Things soon got worse. Indians already living nearby distrusted these newcomers and drove them away. The hungry, homeless Aztec had to beg for land from the king of the powerful Culhua people, who despised them as "great villains."[2] He finally allowed them to settle in an isolated region famous for being infested with snakes. Desperate to survive, the Aztec ate the reptiles.

The Promised Land

Considered barbarians, weaker in numbers and goods than any other group in the great Valley of Mexico, the Aztec did not lose faith in their destiny. They became fierce warriors, hiring themselves out to fight battles for the Culhua. To prove their worth, they presented their employers with stacks of ears cut off dead or captured enemies. They did not exactly thrive, however. They lived in the swamps and reedbeds at the edge of Lake Texcoco. The small, barren islands there had not attracted any other settlers.

But their god had not deserted them. According to a priest of this miserable but stubborn people, Huitzilopochtli ordered them to start building a city in the 1320s. An eagle perched upon a cactus would indicate the sacred site. When they saw this scene the very next day, the Aztec regained their sense of purpose. Many years later, Templo Mayor would be built precisely on this spot.

Now began the long process of building a strong, prosperous state. Soon, Aztec wives and daughters were paddling canoes to the markets of neighboring lakeside towns to sell water plants, fish, birds, and frogs. The men began to construct chinampas, the first of the emerald-green garden islands that would amaze Cortés and his men. A second city, Tlatelolco, was founded.

By 1375, the Aztec enjoyed a degree of prosperity. They also became wiser in the customs of their neighbors. To make themselves more respectable, they chose leaders who had Culhua blood. As the years passed, intermarriage and trade brought peace between the Aztec and the other peoples who lived beside Lake Texcoco.

But the followers of Huitzilopochtli were not content. Once again, they became prized as hired troops for a stronger tribe, the Tepanec. Their skills on the battlefield would earn them the first opportunities to fulfill the promises made by priests around the campfire in the long years of wandering from the forgotten island in the north.

The Foundations of the Empire

The Aztec were convinced that their gods would someday help them—as Huitzilopochtli promised—"conquer all peoples of the universe."[3] According to

Aztec historians at the time of Cortés, their troops fought so hard for the Tepanec in the late 1300s that they were given the right to conquer land for themselves. Gradually, they gained valuable farmland by defeating smaller groups in the Valley of Mexico. The Tepanec sometimes shared the spoils of war with the Aztec. Tribute (payments made to acknowledge submission) in crops, crafts, and slaves were regularly paid to the Aztec by all the people they conquered.

It was not enough. When Maxtla, an especially brutal ruler, seized the Tepanec throne by killing his brother, the Aztec of the island city of Tenochtitlán began to plot with mainland groups to destroy their patrons. In what became known as the Triple Alliance, Tenochtitlán joined with the cities of Texcoco and Tlacopan to attack the Tepanec. A battle raged for 114 days before the city was taken.

As the three victors shared the fruits of victory, Aztec society changed dramatically. According to tradition, the common people had been afraid to join the scheme against the dominant Tepanec. The soldiers got them to agree to participate by offering a strange bargain: "If we are unsuccessful in our undertaking, we will place ourselves in your hands that our bodies may sustain you, and you may thus take your vengeance and devour us in dirty and broken pots."[4]

Impressed by such courage, the people agreed to declare war. They also offered their own bargain: "And thus we pledge ourselves, if you should succeed in your undertaking, to serve you and pay tribute, and be your laborers and build your houses, and to serve you as our true lords."[5]

Perhaps this story was more legend than fact, but it summed up the relationship that existed between the nobility and the common people of Aztec society during Montezuma's reign. Any land that was conquered by the warriors was given either to the ruler or to a member of the nobility. Commoners were tied to these lands. They were expected to serve the upper classes and pay tribute. These farmers and their families were not free to move from one area to another.

Meanwhile, the three cities continued to work together to build an empire, although Tenochtitlán was by far the most important member of the alliance. Having risen against their Tepanec masters, the Aztec were determined that no conquered people would ever rise against them. The empire was strictly controlled, at least in the regions nearest the capital. Any town that did not pay its required tribute would be punished.

Rebellion was further discouraged by the Aztec's many wars of conquest. As the rugged, sometimes ruthless, Aztec armies marched back and forth across the Valley of Mexico, the unarmed farmers they passed working in the fields were constantly reminded of Tenochtitlán's great power. The farmers might be poor, but they were protected from attack by groups that lived by making raids on unprotected towns. The Aztec state was all-powerful.

Hunger of the Gods

Terror was also used to prevent uprisings. A main goal of warfare was to bring back victims for sacrifice. After a successful military encounter, long lines of enemy captives were led back to the capital.

There, an impressive ceremony would remind everyone, friend and foe alike, of the defeat of the Tepanec that had started the growth of the empire. When the Tepanec leader Maxtla was captured, he was sacrificed on an altar. His blood was thrown in the four directions of the compass, fertilizing the land for the next growing season. This ritual also showed that the Aztec now owned the land and its produce.

In later years, captured warriors were subjected to another form of sacrifice. Tied to a stone post, they were given mock weapons made of wood for a battle to the death with an Aztec warrior armed with a javelin or a war club with a sharp obsidian blade. If the captive was strong or clever enough to defeat this fully armed opponent, a second warrior was sent to attack him, then a third, and finally, a fourth. If he outlasted all four, his reward was to be executed by someone costumed as Huitzilopochtli. According to the priests, this form of death was a very high honor.

The groups that were forced to pay tribute to their Aztec conquerors both feared and hated the constant demands to supply young, attractive victims for sacrifice in the capital. It was the future of their towns and cities that helped make up the total of about twenty thousand sacrifices each year.

This Aztec altar was found during the construction of Mexico City's subway system.

Bitter and angry, those under Aztec domination watched silently as the Spanish conquistadors appeared and strode confidently toward the great palace of Montezuma. This *tecpan*, as the palace was called, was faced with black stone, jasper, and alabaster and had three courtyards. Its inside walls were painted with brilliantly colored scenes. It had wooden ceilings and mats on the floor made of feathers, cotton, or rabbit fur.

These pale, bearded men with their steel swords and horses would change the balance of power in the Valley of Mexico. They were clearly determined to exploit the people and their resources. They could be cruel. But their religion did not demand or even allow human sacrifice. This one factor would have a huge impact on the struggles to come. (By coincidence, the god Quetzalcoatl, at least partly associated now in the Indian mind with Cortés, opposed human sacrifice.)

In unhappy towns and cities scattered throughout the Aztec Empire, the subject peoples began to feel a sense of hope. This new feeling was combined with a thirst for independence and for revenge. The people's resentment of the Aztec after years of subjugation made it much easier for the Spaniards to find people to fight on their side as the conflict grew.

Chapter 6

A Harsh Life

[W]ho was not a vassal of Muteczuma [Montezuma]?
—Olintetl, chief of Zautla, upon meeting Cortés[1]

As far as we know today, few, if any, of the Aztec believed in individual freedom. It would have been a frightening idea. No one could survive alone in ancient Mexico. Only as part of a family, clan, and town could one get food, shelter, and protection both from human enemies and from the unpredictable wrath of the gods.

The lines between noble and commoner were strictly drawn. Only a very brave warrior or clever student of the priesthood was likely to move upward on his own merit. Occasionally, a young woman might be allowed to marry into a higher rank of society. But most people lived their lives within their family group and usually on the same piece of land.

Even perfect strangers, such as the invading Spaniards, could tell one class of Aztec from another at first glance. The poor people lived in wattle huts that had walls made of interwoven branches covered with mud. If damaged by rainfall, floods, or rough winds, these walls were easily repaired. Thatched roofs offered protection from the weather and retained heat during the cool desert nights. There was a simple doorway but no windows.

Houses in Tenochtitlán and other great cities were much more impressive. Several rooms were built around a rectangular central court, each with a plastered ceiling supported by a layer of wooden rods. As a safeguard against flooding, the entire structure was built upon a platform covered with a wall of stone. Rooms were set aside for sleeping or socializing, with a kitchen in the back of the house. The number of rooms depended on the importance and wealth of the family, who might need extra space for their slaves or additional storage rooms for their belongings.

Fate alone, everyone believed, decreed whether a child was born into the poor towns of wattle huts, where most Aztec lived and died, or into the very few comfortable, raised houses of the rich and powerful.

Written in the Book

According to the Aztec, the will of the gods was fate. Life was not expected to be easy. Children were told, "Difficult is the world, a place where one is caused to weep, a place where one is caused pain."[2]

Source Document

He who dreamed that the devil calls him, made a vow to him.

He who dreamed that his house burns, it was said, will already die, and if he dreamed that he is swept away by the water, he already will die.

He who dreamed, who saw in a dream that there is singing in his house, it was said, will already die.

And he who dreamed that the mountain crumbles on him, it was also said, will already die. . . . He who dreamed that the sun was eclipsed, it was also said, will go blind or will sell himself.[3]

The Aztec people believed that certain occurrences were predictions of the future, or omens.

The day a child was born, his or her parents quickly lit a small fire to honor the fire god. Then they asked the local priest to look up the birthdate in a "book of fate" or "book of the destinies," the *tonalámatl*. This book was made from Aztec paper, *amatl*, which was made from the bark of wild fig trees. If the day was lucky, a feast was set out and the child was publicly given a name. If unlucky, the celebration would be put off until a better time.

Xochitl, meaning flower, was the most popular Aztec name for a girl, usually coupled with some other name. Boys might be named for a well-liked or famous forebear, just as the ruler of Tenochtitlán was known as Montezuma the Younger. Often, girls were named for their place in the family, such as Eldest or Middle or Only. Boys were more likely to be named after an animal in hopes that they would copy its strength or bravery, or after their date of birth. The early hours of life were considered extremely important. Since Aztec women would spend many hours of their lives making clothing and other fabrics, an infant girl would be handed miniature weaving tools at her name-day feast. Boys, whose future would be spent growing food and defending the country, were handed small farm tools and toy weapons.

The child's life would mimic the lives of his or her parents, grandparents, and ancestors. At age three, girls began to help their mothers with the housework. Chores included the daily baking of fresh corn tortillas and caring for younger children. At the same age, boys began following their fathers to learn about farming the land, hunting and fishing, and making crafts.

Aztec children were known to be obedient, and their parents were patient and loving. Still, it seems that there was the occasional Aztec child who misbehaved or even rebelled strongly against this regulated life. Unruly young children were punished only by scolding. Once they turned eight years old, however, they could be severely disciplined in very painful ways.

A parent might take a spine from a maguey cactus and prick blood from the arms of a rude or lazy son or daughter. In extreme cases, a child would be tied hand and foot and left outside in the cold all night long, perhaps lying in a puddle of mud. Hot chili peppers would be placed on the cookfire to produce smoke that could singe the lungs and eyes. A disobedient child would be held over the fire and forced to breathe the smoke.[4]

But the Aztec who told the Spaniards about these practices did not say they were common. Children usually came to understand that daily work was necessary to feed and clothe the family. Their participation was important. And while children and adults worked together, parents passed down the words of wisdom, the proverbs and tales that were the building blocks of Aztec belief and behavior.

Learning in the World

Such family discussions prepared young Aztec men and women for instruction outside the home. Both types of training had two goals: to teach skills that would be useful to the group, and to implant the idea that each individual must obey the leaders who decide what is best for the entire nation. Each person had a role to play.

Two schools, the *calmécac* and the *telpochcalli*, were set up to educate children. Children could begin school as early as seven years of age or as late as fourteen. All schools were either all-boy or all-girl.

At the *telpochcalli,* or the "house of youth," revered elders taught matters of daily life, from worshipping the Aztec gods with dances and songs to making effective public speeches. Students learned how to make essential and decorative crafts. They were told the ancient stories of Aztec history. Boys learned the arts of war.

A connected school, usually built around a large patio, was known as the *cuicacalli,* or "the house of song." Although students were expected to learn the material word for word, the classes were probably very enjoyable, sometimes even playful. The classes of the cuicacalli were devoted to nonreligious music: love ballads and songs about famous battles or the lives of great rulers and courageous heroes.

Graduates of the telpochcalli would be able to take care of themselves and their families. They would never forget the rituals of the temple. They would also feel proud and honored to be part of an empire that had risen from humble origins to conquer, it seemed, the entire world.

Classes at a calmécac were much more difficult, and the teachers were very strict. Only the upper-class children and perhaps a very few extremely gifted children of commoners were allowed to attend. These were leadership institutions. No one was likely to become a military officer, priest, judge, or member of government without this level of education.

Just as all Aztec felt superior to other peoples, the hardworking students of the calmécacs saw themselves

Students were expected to learn the history of the Aztec people as well as their complex religion and the rituals that were performed at places such as this ceremonial platform.

as worthier than the Aztec masses. Their dedication would open up a world of knowledge: battlefield tactics and mathematics, the laws of the society, and the movements of the stars and planets in the heavens. A Spanish friar observed that "they possessed large, beautiful books, painted in hieroglyphics, dealing with all these arts."[5] Their power as adults would be based upon their control of this body of knowledge.

Because religion was part of every aspect of Aztec life, calmécac schooling included details of mythology not known to ordinary people. With privilege came a price. Students were required to pray often and to participate in other religious rituals. "Every day you will cut agave thorns for penance," fathers told sons entering a calmécac, "and you will draw blood with those spines and you will bathe at night, even when it is very cold . . . [to] harden your body."[6]

If they did not learn their lessons well, the learning and beliefs of their people would not be preserved for future generations. The armies would fail on the battlefield, and the rulers would not store enough food in warehouses to feed the people during droughts or other crises. The songs and dances they memorized were essential for worship services. This music was also important in the major events of life such as weddings and funerals.

Without this knowledge, the sick would not be healed, either. Although women healers visited the huts of the poor and villas of the wealthy during many kinds of illness, trained Aztec physicians may have had special skills. They knew of about twelve hundred herbs or roots that could cure specific sicknesses or lessen pain, how to clean wounds with sap from the maguey cactus and sew them closed, and how to set fractured bones with a splint and plaster cast. A clergyman with the conquistadors wrote, "Some of them have so much experience that they were able to heal Spaniards, who had long suffered from chronic and serious diseases."[7]

Marriage and Family

According to custom, marriages were arranged by the parents of the bride and groom. It was not in the

Herbal medicines were an important part of Aztec health care, and children learned the uses of many herbs in the calmécac.

interest of the community to bring about an unhappy union. The suffering of one couple could infect the health of the town.

The groom, who would be in his late teens or twenty years old at most, and the bride, who might be as young as ten but was usually about sixteen years old, had to agree to the match. That was the ideal. Perhaps an occasional ambitious parent prevented or encouraged a marriage for financial reasons, but the adults involved tried their best to make sure that all weddings were both legal and blessed by the gods. The ward or town council met to approve a young man's choice of a bride.

Religion required that a priest decide whether the proposed marriage was blessed or jinxed by fate. If he decided that the union should go forward, he then carefully chose a wedding date that would bring good luck to the couple.

Married women in the Aztec Empire had the right to own property, sue in court, and sign contracts. In certain very specific cases, a wife could, like her husband, obtain a divorce from the local court.

Otherwise, men held most of the power. It was the husband who was given land to farm to support his family. He could have additional wives, although his first wife and her children were his heirs. Multiple wives were permitted to help women fulfill their roles in society. There was a large pool of unmarried women in Aztec society because so many young warriors died on the battlefield during the continual wars to make new conquests or crush rebellion.

In a new marriage, it did not take long for the customary routines to set in. They did not vary. In the morning, the young wife's first task was to sweep the house and yard, beginning a long day of keeping her family comfortable, well-fed, and clean. She also did the cooking.

Wives spent much of the day spinning thread from cotton or maguey cactus to weave cloth. Some of the material was used to clothe the family, but most was either paid in tribute to the nobility or was traded in the market for foods and other goods. The lady of the house handled all the shopping. From the birth of the first child until her childbearing years were over, she was also responsible for caring for her sons and daughters.

She also took ritual gifts to the temple priests and maintained the family altars to the Aztec gods. The most important of these altars was a small fire that was never allowed to go out. It was considered holy to the Lord of Fire, Xiuhtecuhtli. On other altars, five ears of dried maize were dressed in the image of Xilonen, the goddess who nurtured this essential grain. To keep the young children safe from harm during the dark nights, there was a small stone or ceramic black-painted figurine of Ixtlilton, chief aide to the supreme god Huitzilopochtli himself.

Daily Bread

It was the husband's duty to provide as much food for his family as possible. He farmed, fished, and hunted, and he also found time to make ceramic pots or stone tools for his wife to trade at market. In addition to maize, farmers grew a grain called amaranth, squashes, chiles, red and green tomatoes, peanuts, sweet potatoes, onions, popcorn, guavas, and many other fruits and vegetables.

This life, stable if not luxurious, was often threatened by warfare, unusual storms, earthquakes, or drought. Aztec men and women believed that their hard work would yield little or nothing if the gods became dissatisfied. The tributes paid to the upper classes bought a measure of protection from fate: The nobles who led young warriors into battle would protect unarmed commoners from enemies, and the priests who knew the ancient lore of their religion would know how to please the gods by performing the proper ceremonies at the correct times.

Knowledge and religion were always joined together. In nature, there could always be found elements of the supernatural. The simple folk relied upon experts to explain or soften the harsh realities of their lives.

Even in farming, the tonalámatl (Book of Fate) was consulted because, as one of the Spaniards observed, "the people felt there would be great damage and loss of any crop sown outside of the established order of the days. . . . some signs were held to be good, others evil, and others indifferent."[8] This belief that supernatural forces play a role in every part of life is one of the many factors, including European military technology and Indian allies and disease, that would later be used to help explain why the emperor Montezuma and his great Aztec nation would fall to Cortés and his relatively small band of Spanish conquistadors.

The Fifth World Dies

There will be a Tenochtitlan no longer. It is gone for ever. Turn about, look what is going to befall the Mexica [term for the Aztec].
—A Chalca prophet to Montezuma's court magicians[1]

Montezuma reportedly feared that the world as he knew it might collapse.[2] This was not just because of the coincidence of Cortés's arrival at a moment that was considered sacred to the god Quetzalcoatl. There were other reasons deeply imbedded in Aztec religious belief. Montezuma, as high priest of the empire, was supposed to know every detail of the ancient legends. As in many religions, some traditional stories described the creation of the world and others predicted its destruction.

Drawing upon ideas developed by earlier civilizations such as the Maya of the Yucatán Peninsula, the Aztec believed that the earth had been created five times, making five ages, or five "suns." The first saw plant-gathering giants roam aimlessly, never learning the arts of agriculture or otherwise working. When they were all eaten by a great jaguar, a second age dawned. Again, the humans were imperfect. Magical hurricanes swept across the land, changing them into monkeys. The third age was equally disastrous. Flawed human beings escaped in the form of birds as the world was destroyed by fire. A huge flood ended the fourth age, and its humans became fish.

Next came the fifth age, the world as the Aztec knew it. Its sun was created when a poor but brave god, Nanauatzin, sacrificed himself by leaping into a sacred bonfire in front of all the other gods. A wealthier but slightly less daring god, Tecuciztecatl, jumped in afterward and became the moon. To the Aztec, shadows on the full moon resembled a rabbit; it had been thrown to darken the moon's bright glow so that the night would be restful. At first, these two lights of heaven merely hung in place, but Quetzalcoatl blew them into their orbits with a fierce wind.

Despite the efforts of the gods, the fifth age, too, would be destroyed someday, probably by mammoth earthquakes. The sun of the fifth age, which beamed its life-giving rays on the empire only if it were fed by the blood of human sacrifices, was destined to die out. Montezuma and the Aztec priests tried to read the Book of Fate and the stars in the heavens to predict the exact date of the end.

The Wheels of Time

Of the three kinds of calendars used by the Aztec, the one based on fifty-two-year cycles was most critical in Montezuma's worries about his nation's fate. This calendar was a combination of the other two calendars, a ritual calendar and a solar calendar.

The solar calendar, not unlike the calendars in use around the world today, was based on 365 days. Since each year is actually 365 and a quarter days long, as

The complex calendar was consulted before making many decisions about Aztec life, especially to understand the future.

the Aztec astronomers knew well, they must have had some device like a leap year to keep the solar calendar accurate. The solar year was divided into eighteen months. Each month was twenty days long and was considered to have four five-day weeks. This total of 360 days left five days at the end of the year, a period considered very unlucky.

Naturally, the solar calendar was used to help farmers track and predict the growing seasons. Because specific feasts and other ceremonies were scheduled every year in the same month, this calendar was also important for religious reasons.

The second, ritual calendar was the basis for a complex system of symbols used in predicting the future, but most of that knowledge was lost or destroyed after the Spanish took over. Certainly, no important action was ever taken on a day thought to be unlucky, and religious rituals took place only on the days that were thought to be the most favorable.

Based on a combination of the solar and ritual calendars, each year was given a name and number. The Year of One Reed, when Cortés marched toward Montezuma's island capital, was 1519 in Europe and not considered remarkable for its number alone. Montezuma, however, saw terrible meaning as his solar and ritual calendars meshed together and the future drew closer in the fourth year of his reign, or 1507 in European terms.

That year was the end of a fifty-two-year cycle. The priests of the temples warned that the world was likely to end. During the five unlucky days at the end of this year, all fires throughout the Valley of Mexico were put out and all household possessions were tossed into Lake Texcoco.

At midnight on the last night of 1507, the emperor of the Aztec and the people of Tenochtitlán waited nervously atop the Hill of the Star, the steep crater of an extinct volcano near the capital. Suddenly, a group of stars moved into view, perhaps the Pleiades. A frenzied celebration began: The world would continue. A captive was sacrificed on the altar, and a fire was started on a board on his abdomen. That fire was used to light torches that were sent throughout the valley, lighting new hearth fires, and the next fifty-two-year-long cycle began.

And yet all was not well. Various towns revolted against the Aztec Empire and had to be put down savagely. Thousands of captives were killed in sacrifices at the Templo Mayor. Montezuma knew that previous nations in the valley had disappeared centuries before, leaving little behind but their deserted pyramid temples and strange carvings. He and his priesthood were determined to prevent this fate, if possible.

Sentinels of the Supernatural

The tens of thousands of educated, dedicated priests of the Aztec religion, both men and women, now watched ever more intently for signs of divine guidance. According to one of their followers in Montezuma's day, a priest is wise and "the tradition, the road; the leader of men, a mover, a companion, a bearer of responsibility, a guide."[3] The Nahuatl term for the most important priests, the *tlamacazqui*, meant giver of things.

These servants of the high gods were active in almost all areas of life. When the medical skills of the physician failed, a priest might diagnose the disease as punishment for sin against the gods. The sufferer was required to confess and make offerings in the temple. Or the priest might suspect that a patient had been put under a sorcerer's spell. In that case, the curse would be lifted if the patient drank some unpleasant substance, perhaps skunk's blood, and carried around a piece of jade or quartz.

In the schooling of their teen years, priests had learned to foresee and explain the future. As adults they might eat peyote or other trance-producing substances, hoping that their drugged visions would provide insights into the will of the gods.

Able to read and write the picture-writing used in the all-important calendars and religious manuscripts, they worked constantly to prevent disasters by pleasing the gods. Often they went without food for days at a time while they forced themselves to stay awake, scanning the night skies for divine messages. To remain pure, they bathed frequently and ate very little.

The sacred temple fires had to be kept burning without stop. Prayers and ritual offerings of food were scheduled at specific times throughout the day, and the rooms of the temples were heavily clouded with the fragrant smoke of incense. For the many special religious celebrations, the priests organized the processions and led the chants and dances. They made certain that the young men and women who dressed as gods behaved in the right manner and wore the correct costumes.

Practiced in the arts of human sacrifice, they often sacrificed their own blood to the gods. Carvings show priests stabbing their earlobes with ritual knives or nicking their arms, legs, and other body parts with sharpened spines of maguey. The dried blood, which matted in their long, uncut hair, and the scabs visible

These carvings at Tenochtitlán remind us of the rich Aztec culture and religious life that was practiced before the arrival of the Spanish.

all over their bodies proved that they devoted their lives to religion.

Such men and women, it seemed, would know more than anyone else about the fate of the empire. As more and more strange reports flooded into Tenochtitlán, where five thousand priests tended the Templo Mayor, the combined wisdom and experience of their leaders focused on finding the truth.

Montezuma was both head priest and ruler. There was no separation between religion and government in Aztec life. Therefore, Montezuma relied upon spiritual and political advisors to help him make decisions.

But the ancient lore of the temple did not record any period as disturbed and disturbing as the years after the beginning of the new fifty-two-year cycle. This should be a new era of hope and peace. It became instead a time for worry and confusion.

The Dangerous Game

A decade after the midnight vigil atop the Hill of the Star, Cortés would walk boldly into the presence of the great king. He was following the example of other conquerors from Europe: Strike at the king, and win the empire. Montezuma, who was experienced in dealing with other rulers, knew that Cortés, despite friendly messages sent from the road, was not a peace-loving leader.

Cortés argued and fought his way through hostile towns, making new allies—enemies of the Aztec—to help him invade Tenochtitlán. While alternating between inviting the Spaniards to visit and warning them to go away, Montezuma tried to keep Cortés and his conquistadors from arriving at Tenochtitlán.

One of Cortés's letters to Emperor Charles V of Spain shows this two-sided deceit. As the conquistador made his way steadily toward Lake Texcoco, he escaped a plot by the leaders of one small city to kill him. Montezuma, he knew, was behind the attempt. Still, as he explained to Charles V,

> I spoke to the messengers of Muteczuma [Montezuma] who were with me of the treachery which was planned against me in that city, telling them that the rulers insisted that it had been done by Muteczuma's advice, but that I could not think that such a powerful prince would send me such honored messengers to declare his friendship and at the same time covertly attempt to injure me by another's hand, so that if things did not turn out as he had thought he might escape the blame.[4]

In other words, Cortés proved to Montezuma that it would be very difficult to outfox or murder him. He also hinted that he knew the Aztec emperor was guilty of betrayal but was willing to pretend otherwise.

Montezuma must have thought deeply about this message as the Spaniards, their horses, and their new Indian allies from Tlaxcala headed for the great causeway that connected the mainland to the island capital.

Guests of the Empire

To enter Tenochtitlán, Cortés and his four hundred or so Spaniards marched over a five-mile-long causeway that was so wide that eight men on horseback could ride comfortably side-by-side. Tens of thousands of the Aztec canoed up to the causeway to get their first glimpse of the terrifying strangers. The stories of their

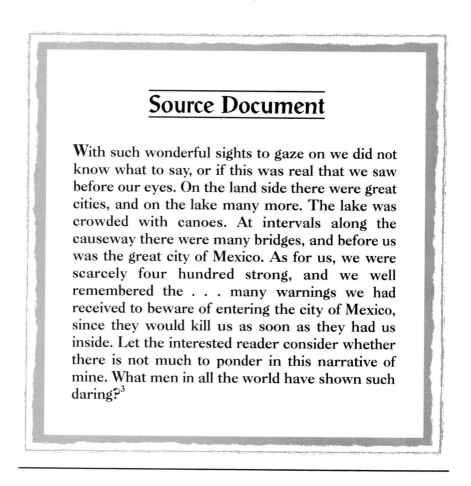

Source Document

With such wonderful sights to gaze on we did not know what to say, or if this was real that we saw before our eyes. On the land side there were great cities, and on the lake many more. The lake was crowded with canoes. At intervals along the causeway there were many bridges, and before us was the great city of Mexico. As for us, we were scarcely four hundred strong, and we well remembered the . . . many warnings we had received to beware of entering the city of Mexico, since they would kill us as soon as they had us inside. Let the interested reader consider whether there is not much to ponder in this narrative of mine. What men in all the world have shown such daring?[3]

Bernal Díaz, one of the conquistadors with Cortés, wrote this account of the Spaniards' first entrance into Tenochtitlán.

cruelty, including the bloodbath in nearby Cholula, had spread like wildfire.

When the Spaniards set foot in the city, tens of thousands more Aztec pressed forward to see them, then parted as their great emperor appeared on foot, shaded by a beautiful canopy held by nobles. He courteously greeted the man whose coming he had dreaded for so long.

Experts still debate the reason behind this polite, humble greeting. Was Montezuma playing a game, or had he really given up? Was he planning to ambush the Spaniards once he had them in his well-armed and well-populated city, or was he marking time until the will of his gods became more obvious to the priests at Templo Mayor? Perhaps, for the moment, he was simply welcoming important state visitors in the traditionally modest way of Mesoamerican rulers.

Since Montezuma did not write down his thoughts, his true feelings and reasons remain a mystery. On the surface, he was a generous host to honored guests. The Spaniards were given their own palace, the home of Montezuma's late father, Axayácatl. It rose beside a plaza in the imperial compound. They were fed with rich foods. Their horses were bedded down on piles of rose petals.

For about two weeks, the Spaniards played the role of tourists. Their host invited them to climb Templo Mayor, with its 113 steps set at a dizzying forty-five-degree angle, so that they could view the panorama of his teeming city. With the permission of the priests,

Source Document

When Motecuhzoma [Montezuma] had given necklaces to each one, Cortés asked him: "Are you Motecuhzoma? Are you the king? Is it true that you are the king Motecuhzoma?"

And the king said: "Yes, I am Motecuhzoma." Then he stood up to welcome Cortés; he came forward, bowed his head low and addressed him in these words: "Our lord, you are weary. The journey has tired you, but now you have arrived on the earth. You have come to your city, Mexico. You have come here to sit on your throne, to sit under its canopy. . . ."

Cortés replied in his strange and savage tongue, speaking first to La Malinche [Marina]: "Tell Motecuhzoma that we are his friends. There is nothing to fear. We have wanted to see him for a long time, and now we have seen his face and heard his words. Tell him that we love him well and that our hearts are contented."[4]

Miguel Leon-Portilla recorded the impressions of the Aztec after Cortés's arrival, including their memories of the conquistador's first meeting with Montezuma.

they were allowed to see for themselves the two huge, bejeweled images inside the two temples at the top of the pyramid, the war god Huitzilopochtli and the rain god Tlaloc. Within these shrines, thick clouds of incense rose from the burning coals upon which roasted the hearts of that day's three sacrificial victims.

Cortés reacted with disgust. "I do not understand how such a great Prince and wise man as you are," he and his conquistadors said to Montezuma, "has not . . . [realized] that these idols of yours are not gods, but evil things that are called devils."[5]

The emperor reacted angrily. "If I had known that you would have said such defamatory things," he snapped. "I would not have shown you my gods, we consider them to be very good, for they give us health and rains and good seed times and seasons and as many victories as we desire, and we are obliged to worship them and make sacrifices."[6]

As the days passed after this event, the Spaniards learned in detail about the system of market days, the class structure of Aztec society, and even the sewage problems. They heard the peppery music of the streets and woke to the drums beating at dawn to welcome the return of the sun, Quetzalcoatl in one of his roles.

But the Spaniards were not idle in their quarters. Taking notes and making plans, Cortés and his men were not distracted from their mission: They were trying to conquer the lands of the Aztec for their Spanish king and convert the people of the Valley of Mexico to the Christian religion.

Then they had an amazing stroke of luck. Given Montezuma's permission to build a church within their borrowed palace, they broke through a wall and accidentally discovered a fabulous treasure—room after room of the gold, silver, and jewelry collected by Axayácatl in his twelve years on the throne. Cortés and his captains "were quite carried away."[7] They quickly sealed up the entrance so that Montezuma would not hear the news. The hoard was richer than they had dared dream. Such a prize stiffened the resolve of even the least courageous conquistador. They must win.

The Sacred Hostage

Montezuma took no steps to protect himself from his armed and reportedly violent guests. His two hundred bodyguards, like everyone else, assumed that no human beings, not even the Spaniards, would dare assault a divine Aztec emperor who had ruled for seventeen years. This attitude was fortunate for Cortés.

Then, as was his nature, he found yet another opportunity in a potential disaster. An Indian uprising began near Villa Rica de la Vera Cruz after two Spanish messengers were killed by one of Montezuma's governors. Soon seven more Spaniards were killed. Cortés put the blame on the emperor.

Backed by thirty of his men, all armed, Cortés strode across the plaza to Montezuma's palace. The conquistador accused him of continuing treachery, and insisted that he come back with his outraged guests to the Spaniards' borrowed palace. Cortés promised the emperor "all liberty," as he put it.[8] The shocking truth, however, was obvious to all: The god-king was under house arrest. This development was a tremendous shock to Aztec morale and esteem.

Years later, Cortés explained his decision to confine his host with a Latin sentence, *"Qui non intrat per ostium fur est et latro."* Translated, this meant "Anyone who does not enter by the front gate is a thief and a robber."[9] Far from sneaking about, Cortés took action in the sight of the entire empire.

For weeks, a peculiar play was acted out by all sides. Montezuma went out in public, but was always surrounded by Spanish guards. Cortés ordered his men to treat their royal captive with respect. He had one man harshly whipped for failing to do so. The two leaders spent time together, sometimes playing games of chance.

At the same time, the Aztec at all levels of society saw that real power had been taken from their ruler. To please his captors, Montezuma ordered the leaders of the revolt near Vera Cruz to come to Tenochtitlán. Cortés had them and their followers seized, tortured, and then publicly burned alive at the stake, a form of execution used often then in Christian countries but only occasionally in Mesoamerica. Montezuma was put in chains to watch as eighteen of his subjects died in the flames fueled by stacks of wooden arrows taken from his palace storehouse.

An unknown native artist depicted Montezuma (right) being taken prisoner by Cortés.

Now feeling certain of their control, the Spaniards became even bolder. After another minor rebellion, Cortés forced Montezuma to call a meeting of his council of elders. Montezuma announced that they were all to consider themselves subjects of Emperor Charles V. The ancient prophecies and signs, he reportedly said, showed that the Spanish ruler was chosen by fate to lead the Aztec Empire.

The cocky Spaniards openly divided the treasure of Axayácatl. Twenty percent went to Spain's Emperor Charles V and 20 percent to Cortés. Common troops received very small percentages, but it was enough to suggest that the future held the promise of greater wealth for all. At Montezuma's request, the royal regalia, made of feathers, was returned to him. His captors were not interested in artistry when they could have gold.

Then, about six months after Cortés marched his men across the wide causeway into the capital, his fortunes veered swiftly and dangerously.

The People Strike Back

With the supposedly meek Montezuma under his control, Cortés bloomed with confidence, to judge from the letters he wrote to his king. No longer did he ask the Aztec for permission to set up Christian altars. Instead, he climbed to the top of Templo Mayor, picked up an iron bar, and as the priests watched in horror, smashed the sacred images of Tlaloc and Huitzilopochtli.

91

"Something must we venture for the Lord," Cortés said, suggesting that he had not paid enough attention to the work of spreading the Christian faith.[10] The stunned priests took their idols down the steep pyramid steps and hid them, never to be seen again by Europeans. Images of the Virgin Mary and St. Christopher were placed atop Templo Mayor.

Cortés had gone too far. Montezuma soon learned that, in revenge, the people, spurred by the priests, were preparing to attack the Spaniards and drive them from the city. Otherwise, they believed, their gods would abandon Tenochtitlán forever.

Cortés tried to stay, but Marina's sharp ears had picked up the gossip of the streets and canals: The Aztec might attack at any time, no matter what Montezuma tried to do to calm them. For his part, the emperor sent his royal axmen to cut wood so that the Spaniards could build three new ships and perhaps sail home to Spain. Meanwhile, the frightened Europeans kept their horses saddled and wore full armor twenty-four hours a day.

The situation grew much worse, but from a different direction. Behind Cortés's back, Montezuma made contact with Pánfilo de Narváez, the commander of a Spanish fleet of nineteen ships that had just landed in Mexico. This expedition had been sent by the governor of Cuba, who was furious with Cortés for disobeying orders and taking control of the Aztec Empire. The governor wanted to be the one to acquire the apparently vast riches held by the Aztec. Narváez and his eight or nine hundred troops were bent on seizing all the power and treasure. The headstrong Cortés and his men were in danger of execution as traitors to the Spanish Crown, if the new Spanish invaders overpowered them and stole their prize.

But once again in a moment of crisis, even when others believed that all hope was lost, Cortés was at his best. According to his own account, he met with his men to discuss the Aztec revolt and the Cuban threat. He convinced them that he could handle the situation.

And so he did. Taking only two hundred fifty of his hardened, experienced troops toward the eastern coast, he made certain that members of the Cuban expedition heard tales about the piles of gold a loyal fighting man could win under his command. For this reason, he met little real opposition from the newly arrived Spanish troops. After only an hour's fighting against his fellow Spaniards, Cortés was victorious. The Cuban troops accepted him as their commander. Narváez, their defeated leader, was jailed in Villa Rica de la Vera Cruz, the town Cortés had founded upon his arrival in Mexico.

Meanwhile, the Spaniards who had been left behind in Tenochtitlán fell into serious trouble. Six soldiers were slain when fifty of them attacked a thousand or so Aztec who were celebrating a pagan festival. The loud music and feverish dancing were interpreted by the nervous Europeans as the beginning of a revolt.

Racing back to Montezuma's royal compound, Cortés tried to restore order, but the Aztec council of elders soon chose another emperor, Montezuma's brother Cuitláhuac. Now the Aztec warriors began to attack with grim intent.

The Fight for Freedom

Today, this uprising against the surprised conquistadors would be called guerrilla fighting. In the small spaces of the streets and squares, the large Aztec population had the advantage over the invaders, who could not effectively use their steel swords or maneuver their large horses. As the heavily armed Spaniards tried at last to leave the city, bands of Aztec warriors attacked from the front and the rear, while bowmen shot arrows from the roofs and balconies. Other warriors slid up the many canals by canoe, suddenly appearing at a bridge or street opening to hurl deadly slingstones. Barricades were hastily set up to prevent the Spanish horses from charging, then the Aztec ran them down, aiming spears into their bellies. The defenders enjoyed a tremendous numerical advantage. If forty of them fell dead in a single charge, thousands more were prepared to take their place.

For the first time since their invasion of the Valley of Mexico, the Europeans were being killed and wounded day after day. Their borrowed palace was assaulted and burned. The new troops from the Cuban expedition were terrified by the daring Aztec, who swarmed over them, shouting threats and beating drums. Cortés himself was seriously wounded in the left hand. Quick to see when a course of action had to be changed, he realized that his forces would be destroyed unless he led them safely out of the city.

Rejected by the Aztec nation, Montezuma could not persuade his people to allow the Spaniards to leave in peace. No longer considered godlike or the true leader of the empire, he was a defeated human being. The former emperor was, of course, most bitter against Cortés. "Fate has brought me to such a pass because of him that I do not wish to live or hear his voice again," he said to messengers sent by Cortés.[11] Fully aware that the Aztec war captains and priests sensed victory, Montezuma believed that the conquistadors would be wiped out soon.

Then Montezuma's sufferings ended at last, although the full story is not clear. Whether forced by Cortés or hoping for an end to the slaughter that ripped apart his great city, he appeared in public and asked the military leaders to call a truce.

Suddenly, the air filled with whistling arrows and hurled stones. Montezuma was hit in three places, including his head. The Spaniards surrounded him and took him out of sight.

Many stories of Montezuma's last days have been told. Most experts believe that he was in terrible pain for three days, refusing to have his wounds treated. After almost two decades on the throne of Tenochtitlán as the guardian of the fate of an empire, Montezuma died on June 27, 1520.

The Spaniards claimed that their leaders, including Cortés, wept at the news of Montezuma's death. Montezuma had been a royal hostage, whom the Spaniards had used as a kind of insurance for their own safety. But he had also proven himself intelligent and wise, even as his world collapsed.

Montezuma's people, though they had removed him from office, loudly mourned his death and swore revenge against the Spaniards. As the Aztec once again took control of the major public buildings and at least half the city's bridges, Cortés planned a night-time escape.

In June 1520, not quite seven months after their triumphant entrance in the bright light of day, the Spanish and their Tlaxcalan allies began sneaking out of Tenochtitlán just before midnight. They were soon caught in an ambush. Fiercely fighting their way to the mainland, they suffered frightful losses during the long struggle, which became known as *Noche Triste*, or the Night of Sorrow. Some two thousand Tlaxcalans and more than six hundred Spaniards were killed or drowned. Many who slipped under the waters of Lake Texcoco were weighted down with gold from the treasure stored by Montezuma's father. The great hoard, weighing perhaps as much as eight tons, sank to the muddy bottom.

Chapter 9

The Great Collapse

They were bent on forcing us to destroy them completely. . . .
All that I could think of was to burn their houses
and the towers in which they kept their idols.

—Cortés to Emperor Charles V[1]

Cuitláhuac was a fiercer warrior than his brother, but he was not nearly as clever. Montezuma, despite fatal hesitations, relied heavily and effectively on reports about the superior battlefield skills and weapons of the armed Spaniards and their horses before making military and political decisions. Another leader might have reacted differently to this information, but Cuitláhuac seems not even to have taken it seriously.

The military lessons of the previous few months were mixed. More than once, the conquistadors had escaped from traps or ambushes and then easily slaughtered Indian troops, even when they were greatly outnumbered. In battlefield skirmishes, they charged astride their horses and mowed down their foes, hacking with steel and firing bullets.

But in the confined spaces of Tenochtitlán, the Spaniards had at last suffered heavy casualties themselves. Now they were on the run, weakened, tired, and low on supplies and food. Aztec warriors armed with slingshots got close enough to Cortés to wound him twice in the head. The army of Tenochtitlán now outnumbered the Spanish invaders by at least twenty to one. Cuitláhuac gleefully assumed that he was on the verge of victory.

The Spaniards retreated for weeks, carefully making their way northward around Lake Texcoco. Sometimes they had nothing to eat but grass. Almost every one of them was wounded. Finally, they rested among their important allies, the Tlaxcala, where they had begun their first trek toward Tenochtitlán.

Meanwhile, Aztec Emperor Cuitláhuac and his advisors felt that the gods were now in control of the situation. Huitzilopochtli, the main Aztec god, would reward the faithful service of the Aztec and their priests.

But Cortés and his men were preparing for their return. On July 7, 1520, Cuitláhuac's followers reported after a horrendous day-long battle that the emperor had seriously misread events. Making a mistake that may have doomed the empire in one battle, Aztec troops lined up in orderly rows in the flat

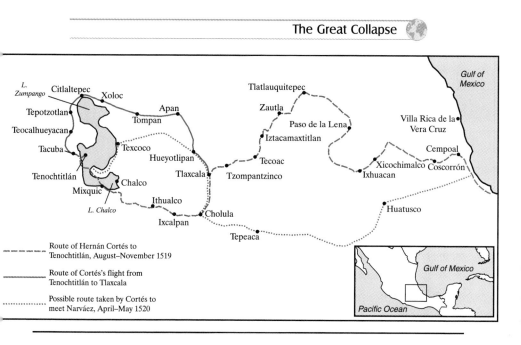

Gulf of
Mexico

L.
Zumpango
Citlaltepec
Xoloc
Apan
Tlatlauquitepec
Zautla
Tepotzotlan
Tompan
Paso de la Lena
Villa Rica de la
Vera Cruz
Teocalhueyacan
Iztacamaxtitlan
Tacuba
Texcoco
Cempoal
Hueyotlipan
Tecoac
Xicochimalco
Coscorrón
Tenochtitlán
Tlaxcala
Tzompantzinco
Ixhuacan
Chalco
Mixquic
Ithualco
Huatusco
L. Chalco
Cholula
Ixcalpan
Tepeaca

Route of Hernán Cortés to
Tenochtitlán, August–November 1519

Route of Cortés's flight from
Tenochtitlán to Tlaxcala

Possible route taken by Cortés to
meet Narváez, April–May 1520

Gulf of Mexico

Pacific Ocean

Cortés made his way back to Tenochtitlán after his defeat by the Aztec, hoping once again to gain possession of the city. This map shows the routes Cortés used throughout his expedition in Mexico.

farmland near the town of Otumba. As Cortés later wrote, they were "so many that in front, rear and on all sides the whole plain as far as one could see was black with them."[2] They advanced with confidence through fields of maize and maguey, and they were soon destroyed row-by-row in assembly-line fashion.

This was exactly the battlefield situation that played to Spanish strength. With their twenty-two remaining horses, their steel swords, their cannons and guns, and their skill at charging into the close-packed ranks of the Aztec and then wheeling off to return again and again, the armored conquistadors smashed the Aztec forces.

Finally, Cortés proved yet again that he could defeat a foe mentally as well as physically. He raced into the thick of the battle to kill the warriors who held high the Aztec emblem, a featherwork banner showing the eagle of the Chapultepec story. When this adored symbol was dashed to the ground, the Aztec troops turned and ran.

Shift in Fortune

From then on, Cortés could not be stopped. After fresh troops and weapons arrived, he marched back toward Tenochtitlán. He was intent on conquering the entire empire with an iron hand.

Terror was again his most important military tool, along with his many native allies and superior weapons. His soldiers quickly defeated the warriors defending the town of Tepeaca, a hilltop fortress. The Aztec survivors and their allies, after being branded on their cheeks, were sold as slaves to other towns or given in service to Spaniards. Within three weeks, Cortés had subdued the entire province.

Slowly, the great engine of Spanish conquest rolled toward Lake Texcoco. Towns that did not immediately surrender were punished. Others nervously pledged their support to Cortés. Horses arrived from the stables of Spanish Jamaica, and Aztec gold was used to buy more ammunition, cannons, and other supplies. Still more soldiers arrived from Cuba and Jamaica and were convinced to help Cortés in his struggle to conquer the Aztec. Cortés ordered thirteen warships to be built for use on Lake Texcoco.

Finally, an invisible but deadly ally joined the Spanish in defeating the native people of Mexico. Its first victim was a Jamaican porter, Francisco de Eguía, who was brought to Mexico by the Cuban soldiers in 1520. Smallpox became a frightening plague almost overnight. Because the disease had existed in Europe for centuries, the Spanish had developed some resistance to it. Usually, it struck Europeans in childhood. It could leave life-long facial scars but generally did not kill. But the peoples of the New World, including the Jamaican slave and the native peoples of the American continent, had never faced smallpox or any other virus. They had no immunity to protect them.

The death toll can only be estimated, since no accurate records were kept at the time. About seven hundred thousand Indians from all groups in the Valley of Mexico died of smallpox by the end of 1521. It was at its worst in Tenochtitlán for about seventy days beginning in mid-October. Sores erupted on the faces, breasts, and bellies of victims. Many who did not perish from disease would die from hunger when there were not enough people to grow and prepare food.

One of those who fell was Cuitláhuac, the emperor. As the Spanish marched toward the capital with greater strength and increased confidence, Montezuma's son-in-law, twenty-five-year-old Cuauhtémoc, was chosen to lead the empire. He would be the last great hero of the Aztec story. On the one hand, his name, which could be translated as "the falling eagle" or "the setting sun," may have been considered a bad omen.[3] On the other, the Aztec calendar had moved from One Reed to the year Two Flint, a lucky year. A flint knife was considered a symbol for the Aztec people.

Cortés Approaches Again

Meanwhile, Cortés moved ever closer. Beginning on December 25, 1520, he led his forces toward the capital, where thousands lay dying or dead from disease. Town by town around the lake, he put down any opposition. Desperate warriors still shot arrows and hurled stones from their canoes. There were many brief, feverish battles, but the Spaniards could not be stopped.

By the spring, Cortés had assembled an enormous force at the shore opposite Tenochtitlán: thirteen warships, about seven hundred infantry, eighty-six cavalry, 118 troops with crossbows and muskets, and about one hundred thousand Tlaxcalan allies.

Divided into three separate groups to attack the causeways to the city and a fourth to man the warships on the lake, this great army would continue fighting for ninety-three days. The fifty-foot-long ships, which could be paddled or sailed, cut off supplies from the mainland. Because the emperor had not foreseen this tactic or prepared for a long siege by filling the city's storehouses, the Aztec defenders had nothing to eat but weeds, roots, and the flesh of their slain companions and sacrificial victims.

The invaders' progress across the three causeways was slow and bloody. During the night, the clever Aztec warriors would dig pits underwater in shallow parts of the lake. The next day, Spanish cavalrymen might sink into these traps, held in place to be slaughtered. The causeways were blocked or broken in places. Stakes were hidden underwater to keep the warships away from the city. The war drums beat constantly, day and night, and the fires atop the temple pyramids showed that the priests were continually calling upon the gods for revenge on the pale intruders. The dead were secretly thrown into backwaters of the lake so that the enemy would not know how many were being killed or were dying from smallpox.

But better equipment, the strong three-pronged invasion plan, the aid of other Indians who hated the Aztec, and the determination of Cortés could not be beaten back, even by warriors willing to die by the tens of thousands. The Spanish commander finally broke into the capital from the south.

The Attack

Once the conquistadors and their hundred thousand or more Indian allies thronged into the city, they had to fight their way down narrow streets, leveling one house at a time. The stench rising from the stacks of corpses was at times overpowering. There were bottlenecks throughout the network of canals because most of the bridges had been destroyed by the defending forces. In close fighting, at least ten Spaniards were captured. They were forced to march up the Templo Mayor to be sacrificed as their fellow soldiers watched in horror a few hundred feet away.

Meanwhile, even as the invaders massacred them, the Aztec refused to give up. They tried to frighten Cortés and his troops by throwing the severed, bloody heads of captured Spaniards at them. But no less cruelly, at least according to Cortés, the Tlaxcalans hacked away at the starving, diseased, terrified occupants of the city, regardless of age or gender. Cortés, characteristically practical, ignored the fact that his allies sacrificed and ate their victims, despite his religious opposition to human sacrifice.

Such butchery and such unequal numbers finally wore the Aztec down. Tenochtitlán had few hiding-places left. There was no rest possible as noise and violence spread everywhere. At last, the survivors of the dreadful siege tried twice to surrender, but they were too late to save the city.

On August 13, with only about an eighth of the capital still in Aztec hands, the Spaniards attacked in full force, killing some fifteen thousand defenders. This was the last battle. By leveling the city, the invaders created the situation that was most favorable to them: Over the rubble their horses charged almost as easily as in an open field of battle. Cuauhtémoc tried to escape to set up headquarters elsewhere to continue the struggle against the Spaniards, but he was captured in his royal canoe. The gold and other valuables that he carried with him were seized.

A Nahuatl poem commemorated this last day of the empire:

Broken spears lie in the roads;
we have torn our hair in grief.
The houses are roofless now, and their walls
are red with blood.
We have pounded our hands in despair
against the adobe walls,
for our inheritance, our city, is lost and dead.[4]

The Last Emperor

Always the politician, Cortés had Cuauhtémoc brought to him with full honors as a head of state. He embraced the Aztec leader with what seemed to be affection, but the shame of defeat was too great for the warrior prince.

"Take that dagger that you have in your belt and kill me at once with it," Cuauhtémoc said, weeping aloud.

Cortés would have none of it. He praised his captive's bravery and assured him that "he should rule in Mexico and over his provinces as he did before."[5] He then ordered his men to take Cuauhtémoc, his family, and his battle commanders with them to the royal compound. Once again, as with Montezuma, Cortés intended to use a great leader for his own ends.

This time, however, he did not have to hide his aims. Cuauhtémoc was imprisoned. Cortés then appointed Don Pedro, the son of the late Montezuma, in his place. The Aztec Empire had been replaced by the colony of New Spain.

Building a Spanish Colony

The excitement of conquest was followed by the necessary work of repairing Tenochtitlán, its farms, and its business. The streets and water system were reconstructed. A weapons factory was built.

But peace was not yet fully restored. Certain Aztec leaders were hunted down and hanged for their part in the revolt. Tired and poor, Cortés's men were eager to get their hands on the fabled Aztec gold. They had long suspected that Cortés had taken a great treasure for himself. Now that they were idle, such suspicions had time to simmer to a boil. Back in Spain, Emperor Charles V was also waiting for his share of the imagined hoard. Charles had received periodic reports from some of Cortés's men, but he remained uninformed of the actual wealth that could be taken from the Aztec Empire. But even the treasure lost in the lake during the Noche Triste could not be found. The Spanish conquistadors wondered whether the Aztec had retrieved it.

Finally, Cortés was forced to make a public effort to find gold. He brought Cuauhtémoc and his chief advisors together and questioned them sharply. They claimed that no great treasure existed. Then, breaking his promises to the emperor, he had Cuauhtémoc and another great leader tortured until they revealed the whereabouts of more gold.

The heroic Cuauhtémoc tried to hang himself before this humiliation but was stopped. He was then tied to a pole, and his hands and feet were dipped in

Source Document

If Your Majesty chooses to grant me the favors which I asked for concerning that discovery, I will undertake to discover a route to the Spice Islands and many others, if there be any between Maluco, Malaca and China, and so arrange matters that the spices shall no longer be obtained by trade, as the king of Portugal has them now, but as Your Majesty's rightful property. . . . [6]

Cortés's fifth letter to the Spanish Crown requested recognition for his accomplishments in Mexico and offered his services for future expeditions on behalf of Spain.

oil, then set on fire. The other Aztec leader was given the same treatment. Both were left crippled for the rest of their lives. In the end, Cuauhtémoc would only mutter that some gold had been thrown into Lake Texcoco when the gods told him that Tenochtitlán would fall to the Spaniards. A little treasure was indeed found at the spot.

The conquistadors were still not satisfied with the amount of gold found. They believed that Cortés had a secret treasure of gold bars melted down from Aztec jewelry. Like other conquerors who seized power in the capital of an empire, he began organizing assaults on other cities of the empire to keep his fellow conquistadors busy. They would, in time, learn that slaves, land, and titles can be much more valuable in the long run than shiny metals.

Cortés After the Conquest

Four years after the conquest of Tenochtitlán, Cortés headed an expedition into the area known today as Honduras. He took along Cuauhtémoc, then accused him of plotting a revolt there. The truth about the whole affair is not clear. Perhaps Cuauhtémoc was simply no longer needed. The Spaniards reported that they hanged their treacherous royal captive.

A local Indian account of the emperor's end told a slightly different story: "On the third day, after having baptized him, [the Spaniards] cut off his head, and stuck it on a tree."[7]

Almost Forgotten

Would that one lived forever; would that one were not to die!

—Nezahualcoyotl, king of Acolhua, a city on
Lake Texcoco's eastern shore[1]

In death, the *teyolia*, or soul, of the last Aztec emperor was supposed to have joined the hundreds of thousands of his people already killed by the invaders in one of three major kingdoms of the dead. The population of each afterlife was determined by how the souls died.

All warriors killed by an enemy or sacrificed on an altar to the gods, including Cuauhtémoc, went to Ichan Tonatiuh Ilhuicac, the "home of the sun in the sky."[2] There, they became the attendants of the sun, serving for four years. Then they returned to the delights of Earth as butterflies or hummingbirds, darting cheerfully about in the subtropical sunlight.

The souls of women supposedly took the same journey if they died giving birth.

In Tlalocan, a fertile paradise ruled over by the rain god Tlaloc, the souls of men and women alike paraded through gardens filled with bright flowers and fresh fruits. They were there because they had died

Tlaloc, the rain god, was believed to rule over one paradise of the Aztec afterlife.

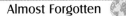
within the rain god's earthly domain of rainfall, storms, and bodies of water—electrocuted by lightning, attacked by a water mammal, or drowned.

The third afterlife, Mictlan, was the most heavily populated. It was the home of everyone who died of natural causes.

Before reaching its fated home, each teyolia on the way to Mictlan passed through nine levels over a period of four days. These stages of the final journey might have symbolized the nine hours of night on the Aztec clock, since death is the land of night. Or they might stand for the nine months that a human child grows in its mother's womb.

The stages were fearsome. At one, for example, the soul had to pass between two mountains that smashed against each other. At another, the fierce, freezing winds threw obsidian knives and stones at it. But every Aztec soul found its way at last to the throne of the Lord of the Dead. It presented the gifts that had been laid beside the body by family and friends at the funeral four days before. In one of the nine regions of Mictlan, as assigned by the god, the spirit would remain for eternity.

Vanished Glory

Destroying such beliefs was, for the Spanish missionaries and their successors in the clergy, more important than destroying the military power of the Aztec Empire. As more of them arrived in New Spain (the colony Cortés built in Mexico), they made the

These Aztec ceremonial grounds, near a Spanish cathedral, vividly show how the Spaniards forced their culture upon the native people of Mexico, although the Aztec managed to maintain some aspects of their own unique culture.

Aztec tear down their temples and use the stones to build churches. They organized schools to teach the beliefs and moral values of Christianity. They demanded that Aztec men wear European-style trousers.

Meanwhile, the Indians were forced to work in mines or on the plantations given to the victorious Spanish soldiers. Except for some Tlaxcalans who had helped Cortés defeat the Aztec, Indians in the Valley of Mexico lost the guaranteed hereditary title to the farms of their families. Although they were legally considered subjects of the new colony, not slaves, they now worked the land not for themselves but for the benefit of Spanish overlords.

At first, Spain publicly ordered the conquistadors of New Spain to educate the Indians and train them for the benefits granted to subjects of the Spanish Empire. But in 1588, the imperial power was greatly weakened when the English defeated its huge war fleet, the Spanish Armada. Messages from Europe could no longer make their way across the Atlantic to Mesoamerica. The Spaniards who ruled the colony did not exactly follow the express wishes of their ruler in regard to his new subjects. Instead, many of the victors devoted themselves to getting as rich and powerful as possible through the work of the Indians who served them.

Only a few Indian groups escaped total domination. Many small groups had taken to the mountains long before, despising the rule of the Aztec and other large Indian states. The Spaniards did not seek them out, nor did they bother a few other groups who lived on land that was not rich or productive.

Cortés—Later Years

During these years, the famous Cortés himself was slowly pushed out of power by his many jealous enemies from Spain. His countrymen quickly forgot the glory of his achievements. His king appointed a new governor to take charge of New Spain. When Cortés went home to Europe, Emperor Charles V sharply made it clear that he was tired of hearing Cortés's requests for more honor and power.

The aging conquistador retired bitterly to a small town near Seville. He died on December 2, 1547, at age sixty-two, almost exactly twenty-seven years after he assembled his great army, and against great odds, marched stubbornly back toward Lake Texcoco to conquer Tenochtitlán. His body would be taken from Spain to Mexico two centuries later and buried with belated honors.

The Aztec After the Conquest

In New Spain, on the surface, the ancient Aztec ways were being forgotten, but the gods were remembered in the towns of the mountains and in the huts of plantations. Each family among the common people lived, as always, on one plot of land, making crafts or growing food that was now sent to Spanish overlords instead of to Aztec nobles. Some Spanish missionaries

*Hernán Cortés is still remembered for the bravery and the brutality
he showed in his conquest of the Aztec Empire.*

looked the other way when pagan music or gods found their way around the edges of Christian worship.

Gradually, the children of the Aztec and the Spanish married each other. The ideas and arts of each culture blended with the other. The people became known as mestizos. New Spain became Mexico, a nation unlike any other, in which the mix of people and culture has brought both color and instability over its more than four-hundred-year history.

Mexico—Later Years

Mexico, which gained its independence from Spain in the nineteenth century, went through many years of political turmoil. The Mexican Revolution of 1910 was supposed to pave the way toward democracy, a process that continues today. It also freed the people of Mexico to look at their past and decide for themselves what was most precious to them.

And so the Aztec and their doomed rulers returned to the scene. Three great Mexican artists—Diego Rivera, José Clemente Orozco, and David Alfaro Siqueiros—began painting world-famous murals in the 1920s, epic scenes that could be seen and understood by the common people. After four and a half centuries of Christian art painted in Spanish styles, these artists and others decided that revolution demanded a completely new kind of art: Mexican and pagan.

Suddenly, the old days of the Aztec were back, at least in the bright colors and monumental figures

Sculptures at the Templo Mayor in Tenochtitlán, which is now Mexico City, show the rich legacy of the Aztec people.

created by these muralists. Ancient warriors and farmers, idols of the fallen gods, and other images of the vanished empire sprang into life. The paintings were more vivid than the old Christian murals in the churches. They showed the common people as strong and courageous. Cuauhtémoc was portrayed as a hero.

The legacy of Tenochtitlán now lives on in other ways, too. Experts have learned how to read much of the Aztec picture-writing found on temple walls and monuments. Archaeologists continue to make discoveries as they look for clues about Aztec life in ruins and gravesites. About a million Mexicans still speak Nahuatl, the language of the Great Speaker, Montezuma. Since the 1970s, scholars have been studying documents written in Nahuatl during the early years of New Spain. Pictures of daily life from the native point of view are changing the standard history of the period.[3]

The living heritage of the small, despised tribe who became a great empire will change with time, but it seems to be growing stronger. This spirit was perhaps best captured on a memorial plaque set up in Mexico City in 1965:

On the 13th of August in 1521,
heroically defended by Cuauhtémoc,
Tlatelolco fell to Hernán Cortés.
This was neither a triumph nor a defeat,
it was a painful birth
of the mestizo people
who are the Mexico of today.[4]

Timeline

ca. **650**—The great city of Teotihuacan mysteriously begins to decline; Its people continue moving away for the next two hundred fifty years.

1111—The ancestors of the Aztec begin their wanderings in the Mexican desert.

ca. **1250**—The Aztec tribe settles in the Valley of Mexico.

1325—Tenochtitlán is founded on an island in Lake Texcoco.

1367—Acampichtli becomes the first emperor, or tlatoani, of the Aztec.

1428—Texcoco and Tlacopan join with the Aztec in the Triple Alliance.

1440—Montezuma I, greatest of all Aztec emperors, takes supreme power.

1469—Axayácatl, father of Montezuma II, becomes emperor.

1486—Ahuítzotl, uncle of Montezuma II, becomes emperor.

1487—Templo Mayor, the largest temple in Aztec history, is completed in the capital and dedicated with the sacrifice of perhaps twenty thousand captives.

1492—Christopher Columbus lands in the West Indies.

1500—Tenochtitlán suffers a disastrous flood.

1502—Montezuma II is chosen to succeed his uncle as emperor.

1519—*February 10*: Hernán Cortés begins his expedition to Mexico.

1520—Cuitláhuac is elected to replace Montezuma; Montezuma dies on June 30.

1521—*August 13*: Tenochtitlán falls to the Spanish and their Tlaxcalan allies.

1525—Cuauhtémoc, who became emperor after Cuitláhuac's death from smallpox in 1521, is executed.

1535—Mexico officially becomes a Spanish colony.

1547—Cortés dies in disgrace in Spain.

Chapter Notes

Chapter 1. The Year of One Reed

1. Tim Wood, *The Aztecs* (New York: Viking Penguin, 1992), p. 8.

2. Personal letter of Peter van der Loo, April 25, 2000.

3. Hugh Thomas, *Conquest: Montezuma, Cortés, and the Fall of Old Mexico* (New York: Touchstone, 1993), p. 188.

4. Ibid., p. 418.

5. Jose de Acosta, "Human Sacrifice Among the Aztecs, c. 1520," *Eyewitness to History*, ed. John Carey (New York: Avon Books, 1987), p. 87.

6. Michael E. Smith, *The Aztecs* (Cambridge, Mass.: Blackwell Publishers, 1996), pp. 164, 265, 270.

Chapter 2. The Great Speaker

1. Richard F. Townsend, *The Aztecs* (London: Thames and Hudson, Ltd., 1992), p. 205.

2. Hugh Thomas, *Conquest: Montezuma, Cortés, and the Fall of Old Mexico* (New York: Touchstone, 1993), p. 45.

3. Ibid.

4. Ibid., p. 21.

5. Ibid., p. 50.

6. Ramon Eduardo Ruiz, *Triumphs and Tragedy* (New York: W. W. Norton and Company, 1992), p. 47.

7. Thomas, p. 19.

8. Ibid., p. 124.

Chapter 3. A Minor Noble

1. Ramon Eduardo Ruiz, *Triumphs and Tragedy* (New York: W. W. Norton and Company, 1992), p. 41.

2. Hernando Cortés, *Five Letters of Cortés to the Emperor,* ed. and trans. J. Bayard Morris (New York: W. W. Norton and Company, 1969), p. 34.

3. Hugh Thomas, *Conquest: Montezuma, Cortés, and the Fall of Old Mexico* (New York: Touchstone, 1993), p. 119.

4. Ibid., p. 129.

5. Ibid., p. 120.

6. Henry Steele Commager, ed., "Privileges and Prerogatives Granted to Columbus, April 30, 1492," *Documents of American History* (New York: Appleton-Century-Crofts, Inc., 1958), vol. 1, p. 1.

7. Thomas, p. 172.

8. Ruiz, p. 44.

9. Hernán Cortés, *Letters From Mexico*, trans. and ed. Anthony Pagden (New Haven: Yale University Press, 1986), p. 30.

Chapter 4. The City of Dreams

1. Bernal Díaz del Castillo, *The Discovery and Conquest of Mexico*, trans. A. P. Maudslay (New York: Farrar, Straus and Cudahy, 1956), pp. 190–191.

2. Michael E. Smith, *The Aztecs* (Cambridge, Mass.: Blackwell Publishers, 1996), p. 45.

Chapter 5. The Place of White Herons

1. Richard F. Townsend, *The Aztecs* (London: Thames and Hudson, Ltd., 1992), p. 56.

2. Michael E. Smith, *The Aztecs* (Cambridge, Mass.: Blackwell Publishers, 1996), p. 44.

3. Townsend, p. 56.

4. Ibid., p. 68.

5. Ibid.

Chapter 6. A Harsh Life

1. Hernando Cortés, *Five Letters of Cortés to the Emperor,* ed. and trans. J. Bayard Morris (New York: W. W. Norton and Company, 1969), p. 39.

2. Hugh Thomas, *Conquest: Montezuma, Cortés, and the Fall of Old Mexico* (New York: Touchstone, 1993), p. 30.

3. Thomas H. Frederiksen, "Aztec Religion—Omens and Dreams," *Student Teacher Resource Center*, 1997–99, <http://northcoast.com/~spdtom/a-omen.html>, (September 15, 2000).

4. Michael E. Smith, *The Aztecs* (Cambridge, Mass.: Blackwell Publishers, 1996), p. 137.

5. Ibid., p. 138.

6. Thomas, p. 507.

7. Smith, p. 262.

8. Richard F. Townsend, *The Aztecs* (London: Thames and Hudson, Ltd., 1992), p. 125.

Chapter 7. The Fifth World Dies

1. Hugh Thomas, *Conquest: Montezuma, Cortés, and the Fall of Old Mexico* (New York: Touchstone, 1993), p. 270.

2. Ibid., pp. 272–273.

3. Richard F. Townsend, *The Aztecs* (London: Thames and Hudson, Ltd., 1992), p. 195.

4. Hernando Cortés, *Five Letters of Cortés to the Emperor,* ed. and trans. J. Bayard Morris (New York: W. W. Norton and Company, 1969), pp. 59–60.

Chapter 8. The Gods Meet

1. Hernando Cortés, *Five Letters of Cortés to the Emperor,* ed. and trans. J. Bayard Morris (New York: W. W. Norton and Company, 1969), p. 71.

2. Ibid.

3. Bernal Díaz, "The Conquistadors Enter Mexico City, 8 November 1519," *The Mammoth Book of Eye-witness History*, ed. Jon E. Lewis (New York: Carroll & Graf Publishers, Inc., 1998), p. 113.

4. Paul Halsall, "Modern History Sourcebook: An Aztec Account of the Conquest of Mexico," *Modern History Sourcebook*, August 1997, http://www.fordham.edu/halsall/mod/aztecs1.html (September 11, 2000.)

5. Bernal Díaz del Castillo, *The Discovery and Conquest of Mexico*, trans. A. P. Maudslay (New York: Farrar, Straus and Cudahy, 1956), p. 220.

6. Ibid., p. 221.

7. Ibid., p. 226.

8. Cortés, p. 75.

9. Hugh Thomas, *Conquest: Montezuma, Cortés, and the Fall of Old Mexico* (New York: Touchstone, 1993), p. 307.

10. Hammond Innes, *The Conquistadors* (New York: Alfred A. Knopf, 1969), p. 155.

11. Ibid., p. 165.

Chapter 9. The Great Collapse

1. Hernando Cortés, *Five Letters of Cortés to the Emperor,* ed. and trans. J. Bayard Morris (New York: W. W. Norton and Company, 1969), p. 183.

2. Ibid., p. 124.

3. Hugh Thomas, *Conquest: Montezuma, Cortés, and the Fall of Old Mexico* (New York: Touchstone, 1993), p. 452.

4. Michael E. Smith, *The Aztecs* (Cambridge, Mass.: Blackwell Publishers, 1996), pp. 282–283.

5. Bernal Díaz del Castillo, *The Discovery and Conquest of Mexico*, trans. A. P. Maudslay (New York: Farrar, Straus and Cudahy, 1956), pp. 453–454.

6. Hernan Cortes, *Letters From Mexico*, trans. and ed. Anthony Pagden (New Haven: Yale University Press, 1986), p. 30.

7. Ramon Eduardo Ruiz, *Triumphs and Tragedy* (New York: W. W. Norton and Company, 1992), p. 53.

Chapter 10. Almost Forgotten

1. Michael E. Smith, *The Aztecs* (Cambridge, Mass.: Blackwell Publishers, 1996), p. 272.

2. Eduardo Matos Moctezuma, *The Great Temple of the Aztecs: Treasures of Tenochtitlan* (London: Thames and Hudson, 1988), p. 163.

3. James Lockhart, *The Nahuas After the Conquest* (Stanford, Calif.: Stanford University Press, 1992), pp. 7–9.

4. Moctezuma, p. 172.

Further Reading

Díaz del Castillo, Bernal. *Cortez & the Conquest of Mexico by the Spaniards in 1521*. North Haven, Conn.: Shoe String Press, 1988.

Henty, G. A. *By Right of Conquest: Or with Cortez in Mexico*. Mill Hall, Pa.: Preston-Speed Publications, 1997.

Lilley, Stephen R. *Hernando Cortes*. San Diego, Calif.: Lucent Books, 1996.

MacDonald, Fiona. *Aztecs*. Hauppauge, N.Y.: Barron's, 1993.

Reader's Digest Books. *Mysteries of the Ancient Americas*. Pleasantville, N.Y.: The Reader's Digest Association, Inc., 1986.

Ruiz, Ramon Eduardo. *Triumphs and Tragedy*. New York: W.W. Norton & Company, 1992.

Sabloff, Jeremy A. *The Cities of Ancient Mexico: Reconstructing a Lost World*. New York: Thames and Hudson, Inc., 1989.

Smith, Michael E. *The Aztecs*. Cambridge, Mass.: Blackwell Publishers, Inc., 1996.

Thomas, Hugh. *Conquest: Montezuma, Cortés, and the Fall of Old Mexico*. New York: Touchstone, 1993.

Townsend, Richard F. *The Aztecs*. London: Thames and Hudson, Ltd., 1992.

Wood, Tim. *The Aztecs*. New York: Viking Penguin, 1992.

Internet Addresses

Frederiksen, Thomas H. "Aztec Religion—Omens and Dreams." *Student Teacher Resource Center.* 1997–1999. <http://northcoast.com/~spdtom/a-omen.html>.

Guardado, Katherine, and David Shindle. *Quetzalcoatl: The Man, The Myth, The Legend.* January 30, 1999. <http://weber.ucsd.edu/~anthclub/quetzal.htm>.

Halsall, Paul. "Modern History Sourcebook: An Aztec Account of the Conquest of Mexico." *Modern History Sourcebook.* August 1997. <http://www.fordham.edu/halsall/mod/aztecs1.html>.

Hulse, Ben. "End of an Empire: The Spanish Conquest of Mexico." *The Concord Review.* January 3, 1997. <http://www.tcr.org/mexico.html>.

Johnson, Charles William. "The Aztec Calendar: The Pointer." *Earth/matriX.* n.d. <http://www.earthmatrix.com/serie02/cuad02-1.htm>.

Index

A

Ahuítzotl, 18

Axayácatl, 85, 88, 91, 96

Aztec Empire, 7, 18, 20, 24, 32, 34, 41–42, 43, 56, 59, 65, 69, 73, 77, 81, 91, 92, 111

calendar, 75–77, 78

destruction of civilization, 113–116, 118

family life, 63, 64, 68–70, 71, 114

government, 46–47, 80, 91, 94

history, 6, 14, 50–56, 65, 100

human sacrifice, 10, 11, 12–13, 18, 40, 49, 57, 59, 77, 87, 102, 104

omens, 7, 8–10, 20, 62, 71–72, 74, 91, 101–102

picture-writing, 6, 67, 78, 118

religion, 10, 11, 12–13, 14–16, 18, 20, 45, 52, 54–55, 60, 61, 65, 67, 69, 70, 71, 73–74, 76, 77–80, 83, 85–87, 91, 98, 100, 103, 107, 109, 110–113, 114, 118

resources, 19–20, 32, 42–45, 46, 59, 88, 91, 104, 106

revolt against Spaniards, 93, 94–95, 96, 97–99, 106

society, 17, 18–19, 22, 35, 39–40, 46, 47, 49, 55, 56, 60, 61, 63, 67, 68–70, 87, 89

warfare, 40, 41–42, 53, 54–56, 57, 60, 67, 69–70, 71, 98, 102

C

Charles V, 29, 32, 33, 81, 87, 91, 97, 106, 114

conquistadors, 6, 8, 10, 12, 13, 16, 17, 18, 19, 21–24, 31, 34, 41, 45, 54, 58–59, 68, 81, 83, 84–85, 104

capture Aztec emperor, 42, 88–89, 91, 96

cruelty, 36, 100, 106–108

desire to convert natives, 87, 92

military advantages, 7–8, 34, 35–36, 72, 94, 97–99, 100, 103

retreat from Tenochtitlán, 96, 98

role of Indian allies, 6, 24, 34, 59, 72, 80, 81, 96, 98, 100, 102, 103, 104, 113

role of smallpox, 101, 102, 104

Cortés, Hernán, 7–8, 13, 30, 42, 54, 60, 88–89, 91, 92, 94, 97, 99, 104, 107

approaches Tenochtitlán, 13, 21–24, 34, 38, 41, 58–59, 76, 80, 81, 91, 98, 102, 103–104, 114

connection to Quetzalcoatl, 8, 59, 83

death, 114

expedition to Honduras, 108

fights Narváez, 93

religion, 83, 92

Cuauhtémoc, 101–102, 104, 105, 106–107, 108, 109, 118

Cuitláhuac, 94, 97, 98, 101

Culhua, 53, 54

D

Díaz del Castillo, Bernal, 39, 84

E

Eguía, Francisco de, 101

G
gold, 19, 29, 30, 32, 42, 43, 45, 88, 96, 100, 104, 106, 107–108
Grijalva, Juan de, 19, 29, 32

H
Huitzilopochtli, 51, 52, 54, 57, 70, 87, 91, 98

I
Ixtaccihuatl, 22
Ixtlilton, 70

L
Lake Texcoco, 8–10, 22, 53, 54, 77, 81, 96, 98, 100, 101, 102, 107, 109, 114
Leon-Portilla, Miguel, 86

M
Marina, 30–31, 86, 92
Mayan Indians, 30, 73
Montezuma II, 7, 8, 10, 13, 16, 17, 18, 19–20, 21, 22, 24, 27, 31, 32, 34, 35, 38, 41, 43, 46–47, 49, 56, 58, 60, 63, 72, 73, 74, 75, 76, 80–81, 82–83, 85, 86, 87, 88–89, 91, 92, 94, 95, 96, 97, 101, 105, 118

N
Nahuatl, 10, 22, 30–31, 78, 105, 118
Nanauatzin, 73
Narváez, Pánfilo de, 92–93
New Spain, 105, 111, 113, 114–116, 118
Nezahualcoyotl, 109

O
Oaxaca, 18
Olintetl, 60
Otumba, 99

P
Popocatepel, 22–24

Q
Quetzalcoatl, 8, 14–16, 59, 73, 74, 83, 87

R
Roman Catholic Church, 29, 32–33, 59, 67, 68, 83, 87, 89, 91, 92, 111–113, 114–116, 118

S
Sisqueiros, David Alfaro, 116
slavery, 49, 100, 101, 108, 113
smallpox, 101, 102, 103

T
Tecuciztecatl, 74
Templo Mayor, 40, 54, 77, 80, 85, 91, 92, 104
Tenochtitlán, 7, 8–10, 20, 21, 24, 34, 35, 38, 39–40, 41, 42–45, 46, 47, 49, 52, 55, 56, 61, 63, 73, 76, 80, 81, 84, 89, 92, 93, 95, 96, 98, 100, 101, 102, 103, 104, 105, 106, 107, 108, 114, 118
Tepanec, 55, 56, 57
Texcoco, 40, 55
Tezcatlipoca, 13, 14–16, 18, 20
Tlacopan, 40, 55
Tlaloc, 87, 91, 110–111
Tlatelolco, 54, 118
Tlaxcala, 34, 41, 81, 96, 98, 102, 104, 113
Toltec, 14, 16
Triple Alliance, 40, 55, 56

V
Valley of Mexico, 7, 10, 14, 43, 49, 50, 52–53, 55, 56, 58, 77, 87, 94, 101, 113
Velázquez, Diego, 29, 33–34